T

Jai Arun Ravine

▽ ∞ ✳

ISBN 978-1-937421-18-2

Printed by McNaughton & Gunn
Distributed by Small Press Distribution

Copy edited by
Willow Germs and Madison Davis

TIMELESS, INFINITE LIGHT
4799 Shattuck Avenue
Oakland, CA 94609

timelessinfinitelight.com

# THE ROMANCE OF SIAM

# HINTS TO WALKERS

1.   *Never walk alone.*

2.   *On Easter Sunday afternoon in 1967, [Jim] Thompson,
      the renowned American from Thailand, vanished into the
      jungled mountains of Malaysia's Cameron Highlands. His
      vacation companions at Moonlight Cottage assumed that
      he was off on one of his frequent solitary strolls, but they
      grew alarmed when he had not returned by nightfall. The
      authorities were alerted, but their search parties failed to
      uncover a single trace.*

3.   I am thinking of silk tycoon Jim Thompson's afternoon walk
      into the jungle and his bizarre disappearance as symbolic
      of the desire many White people have to lose and reinvent
      themselves in Thailand. I call this inexplicable phenomenon
      WHITE LOVE.

      This subverted travel guide interrogates WHITE LOVE by
      tracking the ways it proliferates in popular American media,
      mutates as a virus in the industry of tourism, and plays out
      in the theater of the western imaginary. It also examines
      the blurring of fact and fiction and the reinvention of self
      through a kind of acting, which is so often the lure of
      Thailand's landscape.

      WHITE LOVE's obsessive and addictive texture is mirrored
      in my use of the sestina, the form of which replicates the
      need for repetitive patterns and a search for satisfaction in
      affective valences that cannot entirely be grasped.

**INFORMATION:** #2 is from the dust jacket of William Warren's *The Legendary
American: The Remarkable Career and Strange Disappearance of Jim Thompson*
(Houghton Mifflin Company, Boston, 1970).

**DID YOU KNOW?** #1, #6, #7, and the italicized portion of #5 are pulled from a
Cameron Highlands trail marker. See Warren (page 7).

**4.** As a mixed race person of Thai and White descent, my attempts to connect with Thailand as "place" and "cultural identity" are colonized by tourism and White desire. The western imagination has constructed a particular fantasy and romance around Thailand, which is subsequently mass-produced by Thailand's tourism industry for its own profit. For non-Thais (Americans, White people, White men), Thailand's collision of ancient religious tradition and R&R facilitates a sense of freedom and escape, as well as a permission to reinvent self, which translates into its supposed ability to accommodate extremes (i.e. the impossible is indeed possible, only in Thailand).

Despite the fact that Thailand was never colonized by another country, tourism is the occupying force in the country today. The hyper-referentiality and over-saturation of sources, links, quotes, references, actors, and characters that I work with in this project are meant to mimic that colonizing force. In this process, Thailand itself becomes obscured. What is left is Whiteness.

This project attempts decolonization in the face of such an erasure.

**5.** This pocket guide will help you navigate the wild jungle of White desire. Go ahead and lose yourself. Fake your death. Reinvent yourself. *DO NOT PANIC.*

**6**. *You should always take the following items on your walk:—*

    *a. A filled water bottle.*

    *b. A box of matches (to light a signal fire).*

    *c. A compass (this may be bought at the tourist board).*

    *d. A whistle.*

    *e. A torch.*

    *f. A little food (e.g. chocolate).*

    *g. A knife.*

**7**. *KEEP TO THE NUMBERED PATHS AS SHOWN ON THE MAP.*

# WHITE LOVE

*...and, um, as soon as I, I saw the, the word Thailand, I, I knew. It's sort of a, strange feeling, um, to explain...*

- Paige Battcher

# WHITE LOVE

*Why Thailand? I literally looked through the, the catalog once
and, um, as soon as I, I saw the, the word Thailand
I, I knew. It's sort of a, strange
feeling, um, to explain. But I, I went out that night and bought a,
uh, Culture Shock book, um, on Thailand, read it in about
three hours and decided that, you know, everything
about the culture of the people, the history of the place
is something that I, I needed to explore on my own.*

An example of white desire

I, I have never owned the place of my, um, mother's birth. I,
I visited there once, twice and I, I want to apply for the, uh,
Fulbright, too. I, I've read literally everything White people
have written about, um, Thailand but I, I wasn't prepared for
the, uh, shock of being too, um, White, too American, too,
you know, strange

for Thai people. It's sort of a, um, strange feeling for me too,
Paige, that you can own the experience of, uh, being there
and no one's, you know, shocked about it. Everyone else has
been to Thailand at least once: The People Are So Nice. And
The Food!!! I, I see the word Thailand written on overpriced
imported coconut milk cans, uh,

everything except my body has the mark. Your life, and ev-
erything in it changed for you and, um, nothing changed      *alienation*
for me. I, I'm a stranger in a place I, I thought was mine.
*Lonely Planet Thailand* says the Kingdom of, um, Thailand
draws more visitors than any other country in Southeast Asia,

**DID YOU KNOW?** This destination features lines from Paige Battcher's interview on
the "My Fulbright Life" podcast, September 9, 2010.

**INFORMATION:** The Thai title of Apichatpong Weerasethakul's film *Tropical Malady*
(2004) is สัตว์ประหลาด ("strange creature").

while its, you know, own people are drawn to Europe, to study French, and not once do they miss the, uh, virtually irresistible combination of shocking

grandeur and ruin. Culture, um, shock works in many different ways, Paige. I, I pretended I, I couldn't speak English, suppressed everything non-Thai so I, I could, you know, belong? Once my, um, mother said, I, I've lived with strangers all my life, one more won't make a difference. I, I was on my own reading the word, um,

Thailand in books in order to learn about myself, but Thailand *loves* and, uh, *accepts* you without *question* and I, I'm in shock and I, I don't think I, I will, you know, recover, ever. I, I want my own Fulbright Life. I, I want to steal everything you took. *Tropical Malady* or "Strange Creature," um, that's what I, I am. Once

and forever, not just Once In A Lifetime, I,
I want to experience, um, Thailand—
the strange feeling of, uh, amazing shock
to discover that, you know, everything I am
a White person owns.

# THE ESCAPE ARTIST

*a world of make believe*
*sharing your smile it has to be relive the stories of ancient glory*
*now and forever the story*
*never-ending you'll always remember*
*among the miracles waiting for you to share*
*you'll never be the same again the things you see will change*
*you always and forever let our two worlds collide*

*there's wonders to see* abroad. You're in the States and you hate it. You want to collide with the atmosphere of England and believe writing a letter to a British woman will be your escape, the change

promised. You must have picked the most expensive story of them all. Secretarial colleges say, "I will look after you," 42 Snow Hill shares this twentieth instant. The new term begins 3rd September—remember

to bring a Shorthand Fountain Pen for writing circular letters, remember your specimen business and receipts. A British woman's search for a family collides with a dead end and you don't write back to share how you're

getting on. You never talked to her again. You stopped believing it could even be possible, next door in a small commercial motel. The story being you couldn't afford a real crossing of the threshold, *a real change of consciousness, nothing was*

**DID YOU KNOW?** This travel package is the first in a series of sestinas written from lyrics to the featured song in the Tourism Authority of Thailand commercial "Once in a Lifetime" [http://www.youtube.com/watch?v=dUMVYtuqL7o], which is part of the Amazing Thailand campaign. The author is interested in confusing the desire to escape *to* Thailand, as it is produced by tourism, with Thai people's desire to escape *from* Thailand.

**INFORMATION:** The title is taken from a 1982 film based on a book by David Wagoner. A line is taken from Wagoner's *Who Shall Be the Sun?* (Indiana University Press, Bloomington, 1978).

*ever the same again.* Change flirted with you in the creases, in the ink, you wanted to remember something you'd never seen. I don't even know your story and here a British woman knows the states you hated, is surprised, she collides with what you wanted so much to be, she asks you to believe in writing letters to the Thai Embassy in London after she shares that she did everything she could possibly do to share her life at Stoke-on-Trent. Mrs. Principal promises a change,

but you're really looking for an art of escape, believing that there could be a way out through a letter, remember? You collect stamps, plane ticket stubs and luggage. Your obsession with travel collides with the folding and sealing of envelopes. If I ask you to tell a story from 1968

there would be the scratch of a fountain pen. The story would be English and Spelling and a P.S. full of commas. You'd share only a blank sheet of paper folded into an addressed envelope with no collision return, opened on one side with a blunt edge.

Your version of events can't change because there's no archive. When I try to remember you there's just film negative, you standing next to a figure without a name,

so I make believe that I knew you in 1968. All I can do is believe this British woman's story, to remember the one letter she wrote, what you did not share with me, and how all our change collides.

# BACKPACKERS

Every story about Thailand starts with you, a young American backpacker on holiday, walking in flip-flops and cargo shorts and Beer Chang tank tops through markets of bootlegs of bootlegs of tourists, through guesthouses overrun by roaches and beautiful French girls having sex in the next room. You have to turn on the fan just to blow away all the smoke coming off her body. Pull the pin and she's like a smoke bomb for signaling or as a screening device.

With all your boy-scout military backpacking skills, you're handy with pockets and a fantastic guide to getting there and away, to paradise where everything is bootlegged and cheap, where sandwiches and coffee are French and freshly imported. When you light up a roach, you're not thinking about the history of imperialism. Cockroaches scuttle like they do in fiction books on Thailand. "I want to smoke this blow with you," say the French girls, fresh out of the shower. The French girls are filming your next porn film in their minds and the main character is a backpacker: young-ish, American-ish, White-ish, with a bootleg because he has no legs.

The fan has three settings but it's stopped oscillating. Frenetic fan clubs follow you everywhere ever since THE ROACH GUESTHOUSE made it big on the bootleg circuit. Tourists want pirated DVDs made from the bootleg of the novel of the bootleg of smoke. My country is going up in smoke all because of you, backpacker, and because I studied Spanish instead of

**DID YOU KNOW?** "Backpacker," "bootleg," "roach," "French," "fan," and "smoke" are six words taken at random from the first few pages of Alex Garland's novel *The Beach* (1996).

**INFORMATION:** "Of course witnessing poverty was the first to be ticked off the list. Then I had to graduate to the more obscure stuff. Being in a riot was something I pursued with a truly obsessive zeal, along with being tear-gassed and hearing gunshots fired in anger." – Alex Garland, *The Beach*

French in high school. Who colonized more people, the French or the Spanish? Either way, Thailand is in the middle asking for more fans and printing plane tickets and translating brochures badly for backpackers, asking them to go on reckless drunken tuk-tuk rides, even off-trail to get attacked by roaches—all the while blowing smoke up the ass of the fantasy of white sand beaches bootlegged from a movie banned in Thailand, which is a bootleg from America.

But don't worry, we won't forget about the French girl. We know. She wants to bum a smoke.

All we need is a fan, some phosphorescence and the scuttle of cockroaches playing shuttlecock to make you a happy backpacker. Backpackers have bootlegged THAILAND: THE MOVIE, starring roaches and French girls and fans that don't work, obscuring me in smoke.

# CHARTERED ARCHITECT / NEGATIVE ENDINGS

*Reaching for the sky finding the strength to try knowing a helping hand is right there beside you a world of make believe so come and join us it's simple to get here the new and old as one in perfect harmony the world is here leave all your cares behind we know that you will find so many welcome friends before your time has ended*

Before August of 1968 ended, you thought you'd try the UK. A negative spectacle was everything behind, and to go forth all you had to do was believe something would happen, and that harmony could be achieved simply by being in another country.

EMD/EJH on 24th July says, *Simple, I should be very pleased to hear from you ASAP* and ended with *Yours Sincerely.* RA/JAB/315 on 25th July is not harmonious, *We do not accept enrollment for courses by post, try presenting yourself for interview at the College, Yours Faithfully.* Believe in yourself in the present tense and leave the national bank behind.

SHP/NE on 26th July says, *Enter through Prince's Gate behind, Yours Truly,* on Trent and under Lyme. Life at 113/6 was simple, purchase foreign means of payment for taking out in person. I believe you intended pounds but it ended up being the US dollar instead, signature. You tried but where is the school certificate attached?

Pink flowers harmonize with green car hoods, the Port Royal Hotel in harmony with your dream. Potted plants hang behind you in a row and that image is forgotten. One side France, another side Germany... Try to decide, chartered architect of the future. It's simple to blueprint your escape route, certificate of exportation ends 30 days from date of approval.

**DID YOU KNOW?** This travel package features lyrics to the song in the Tourism Authority of Thailand commercial "Once in a Lifetime."

I believe you'd already given up by that point, you believed
taking pictures of the same building with pink trees around it
would bring some harmony to your life, so all I have now are
the negative endings of each shutter, of each seal. Musical
kiosk, Paris Bank behind. You photograph the outside of a
cafe without going in. It's simpler that way, you don't even
have to try.

Trying to believe in a simple harmony
means what gets left behind is your own end.

# BACKPACKERS 2: [WHITE GOES EAST]

When you say Thailand is tolerant of gender variance, you're referring to the "ladyboy" you almost had sex with who turned into a zombie and threw an arsenal of coconut bombs at your head until you went into a coma. You were airlifted in a special issue Orchid helicopter operated by Thai Airways. When you came to, you got a massage ("that kind" of massage) and sat at a table with a tablecloth and silverware in a restaurant catering to White expats and served by zombies.

The real-life star of *Beautiful Boxer* would have been denied entrance because of her symbiotic polarities, but your pet boxer who runs into walls—there's a place setting for him. You think "ladyboys" are so articulate and earnest and innocent, you want to take them out to restaurants to teach them how to use forks and knives, you want to take them home and make them cook with Lite Coconut Milk from Trader Joe's, because the real kind makes you fat. You make them give you massages every afternoon at 3, you make them put tiny little orchids in your cocktails. "Devastating" and "beautiful" are adjectives used to describe orchids and the second kind of woman who finally learns how to be a boxer and defend herself on the street.

The number of White people learning Thai massage makes my back hurt. At the guesthouse there's a sign saying "IF YOU BREAK THE RULES AND BRING 'LADYBOY' WE'LL CHARGE EXTRA IMMEDIATELY 1000 BAHT." Coconut water is so trendy, they serve it at restaurants out of the can. Somewhere in the continental US, a Thai restaurant opens. Several seconds later,

**INFORMATION:** "White Goes East" is a chapter heading in Maurice Collis' book *Siamese White* (Faber and Faber Limited, London, 1936).

**DID YOU KNOW?** This destination references the film *Beautiful Boxer* (2004), about the life of Nong Tum Parinya, a Thai transgender woman (or *sao praphet song*, "second kind of woman") who is also a professional boxer. The guesthouse sign was spotted by the author in Chiang Mai in 2011.

an orchid specialist orders take-out Pad Thai. Later that night young green coconut pulp dries to crust on the specialist's dead body—*CSI: Bangkok.*

After the break, you watch televised boxing matches and buy miniature tuk-tuk cabs made out of recycled Singha beer cans. You think "ladyboys" are one of the most fascinating Siamese breeds. You are the first to declare that, like the orchid, it is a Perfect Hybrid of Both Worlds. I'm going to box the living shit out of the best of both and leave you with coconut-sized bruises on your face, swollen so much like a coconut you'll want me to hack at you just to relieve the pain. A massage would be nicer but I'm not fucking nice, I'm a beautiful boxer and I don't give a shit about your fancy Thai restaurant chain or the new breed of killer orchid steaming up your bedroom like a "ladyboy."

I'm Thailand's # 1 tourist attraction: a "ladyboy" in a coconut milk can imported on Royal Orchid Airways. Excuse me, Sir, chair massage is the only way to fly. Please stow your authentic restaurant inside this box.

eeds some space. He's been having a rough
unctioning in his face, positioning himself
gle, the pressure of saying the right thing
at the right .... ithout ADR.

When Anthony (Tony) is not on television, he's still on television, and last night I watched an anime where someone put his arm into a widescreen TV in a deserted department store and then, his body. This is the Asian influence, or one of the life-changing things, strangely enough, about Asia—the television, the constant flicker, the constant blue-lit reminder.

Tony is constantly on television—breakfast, lunch, and appetizers.

In Tony's television something delicious is seemingly everywhere. Food that's cooked in Tony's television has a destination of Tony's mouth, the end of the line, the train car that smells like wet Doberman with one ceiling fan.

Thai sausage has long been an obsession of his. He already knows what he wants. He'll have one with everything. He'll have everything (He does not ask *Can I?* He does not upward lilt or rising tone mark. He points "one" and then gestures "with everything" so we are meant to understanding his meaning.)

*Demonstrates the inconciderate manners americans have*

All food is destined to be televised in Tony's guts, Tony's gut a minor obsession of the television screen. Hollywood flickers in Tony's gut. The food pretends to be *Fresh! Vibrant! Crispy!* rather than decomposed.

**INFORMATION:** This destination is a parody of Anthony Bourdain's *No Reservations* episode [Season 6 Episode 6 Thailand (2008), Travel Channel]. Some language is pulled directly from Anthony's dialogue.

It need not be reiterated: in Tony's television there are no reservations. Food floats by and by and ends up pixilated in his gut.

Tony makes his home on television. Food gets cable in Tony's guts—Food Network 24/7. In Tony's guts we watch food watch Food Network while it slowly decomposes.

Tony needs some space in his gut. Enough with these televisions! Tony's gut crushes them with enzymes and they shatter. Travel Channel shattering in Tony's gut. Food Network crawling onto lawns and eating people's poodles.

For Tony space is zero point zero production. Space is the space of non-production. Space is no space. And in this space Tony finds himself on television eating something that makes him believe \"nothing else matters.\"

Television is a space inside Tony's gut that is always on. He eats the television, composting into a projected set of color values meticulously edited and re-mastered, his voiceover the omnipotent \"hunger for more.\"

It's a good moment in making television: no plans to shoot anything, and look—\"fish balls!\" It's destiny, and it's all recorded in Tony's gut.

In Tony's televised gut everything is free. Memory is the limit for Tony's gut and expansiveness is a juice on television and whenever I think about the television I think about Tony. I think about what must be reserved (nothing) and then I start eating.

*emphasizes the over accesability*
*of these things for*
*priveledged ppl.*

Some of the eating does not come with a memory. Just a flavor or Tony saying, \"fuck the train.\" Just a chili and those amazing Thai condiments. Confused yes. But in Thailand you don\'t care. In Tony\'s gut you don\'t care. The food decomposing doesn\'t care. There\'s so much space it\'s free and it\'s on television so why would we have to remember at all.

Tony\'s show means I don\'t have to remember. I can watch television to learn what it tastes like, what it could taste like, what there \"might\" exist for me to taste.

*See Thailand and experience it through a screen*

And really I just need the \"idea\" of the taste. A \"picture\" of the taste. Then my gut—just space. \"Space\" space. Then my guts fade to white.

Tony tells me to go out for some wides. I\'m fucking DONE. I\'m done with this place and this gut.

Nothing to do really, but eat.

# SIAMESE GRAND SLAM

*for Tiger Woods, Ronaldo V. Wilson, and our mothers*

We watched Tiger Woods on television because he was half Thai, his mother Tida in dark sunglasses and a big visor keeping the sun out, so Thai, Ronaldo played tennis like I did because it might make you famous, his mother Carmelina threw her bag at a ballerina, my mother's nickname is Daeng, a sound like the smell of rice when you first open the cooker, the steam, Jai

is the word for heart, but my mother won't call me Jai, how did Eldrick Tont become Tiger, kids used to ask if we were related to him, Daeng went to all of my ballet performances, I think, if she met Tida I hope they would get along, at least on the outside, and Carmelina would join and they would watch Tiger on TV together and cheer, Ronaldo

writing his queer brown body poems like Ronaldo does and Jai writing their queer brown body poems like Jai does and all the while keeping our addiction to honey from our mothers, Carmelina shops for clean nice new clothes, the imprint of Tiger in the regal carriage, the exalted station of Tida, who is laughing and making a joke and Daeng

is laughing so hard she's crying, Daeng meaning the color red, a volatile temper, Ronaldo cutting off the excess fat and sucking cock, Tida says, *What the hell is the matter with your ass*, Jai is afraid to inadvertently say the word "ass" in a sentence, Tiger is my brother's role model, I wish he'd stop being an asshole, Carmelina

starts to forget things but has big plans, like Carmelina the opera, a rich idea performed to perfection, Daeng typically likes clean nice perfection, she loves Tiger because he has a Thai mother and Ronaldo is in his mother's sewing room with the texture of encyclopedias while Jai reads dictionaries looking for an entry on themselves and Tida

says, *Why you take yourself so seriously*, hanging up a picture
of her son Tida fell off a table and injured her knee, is Carme-
lina that proud of her son that she would sustain injury, Jai
isn't even a son so how could Daeng be proud at all, Ronaldo
dresses up to perfection but what if we're all tigers—


Tiger flooding Tida's house with gold.
Ronaldo's buttons all in a row. Carmelina
singing an aria while Daeng ignores Jai, on the outside.

# TIGER TEMPLE

*for Tiger Woods, Ronaldo V. Wilson, and our mothers*

Our mothers' mouths are always open. They are always laughing.
We are always thinking of the hook curve of their teeth and the hot
breath behind it. Our limbs dent where we wish they'd touch us.

Their eyes are always twinkling. We sit outside in the dark,
rummaging. Stranded without momentum, they bat at us like
golf balls. We look up at them, majestic star clusters, burning
orange and white.

They mostly ignore us and laugh amongst themselves, some-
times to the point of tears, batting at each other softly and
kneading the floor.

They gnaw at our hard knots. Cuspids pierce us through with-
out puncture. We are cubs again, gnawed on in our mother's
language, furry tongue and its hot cut. They chomp down
and shut us out; we grasp their slippery dreams like tusk.

They bat us away like they don't care.

We go to Tiger Temple to pay respects to our mothers. I prefer
to be with mine, but I can't tell which one is one quarter, one
quarter, and a half.

**DID YOU KNOW?** There's a real Tiger Temple in Thailand.

**INFORMATION:** Some language is taken from "Tiger Woods conquers Thailand, his
second home" by Kristin Huckshorn / Knight-Ridder Newspapers, *San Jose Mer-
cury News* and "Tida in Thailand: To understand the essence of Tiger, you have to
know his mother" by Jaime Diaz, *Golf Digest* (May 2009) [http://www.golfdigest.
com/story/tida].

Tiger has always described himself as half Thai. A mother raises her son and we have Asian mothers. We agree our fathers were less persistent and did not rebirth in tiger.

The whole time we're there, they nap. Danger has no sharp edge, it lopes in soft heavy flesh. Laze. Frail flimsy sticks blur the edge of space. Sleep blurs the frail edge they bat. Soft pad, pat-pat.

We want to loll them into us to feel their belly heat. We practice putting, now and again, when we feel like it. We try calling, but they don't pick up their phones. *My mother never understood me, I tried to break the wall*

*but couldn't.*

*The sense of Thai heritage is so strong.*
*It is so totally Thai, and I believe that for every Thai,*
*whether they know it or not, this music flows through their veins.*
*It is very beautiful and it must be preserved.*
*Lookthung comes from the heart.*
*To sing it well, you have to feel it.*

I'm trying to feel something, but I can't. Are you sure I have
what it takes? I made up my mother's name, I know she's
strong but she keeps hiding. I intercept letters from 1972
and a broken heart. Pamplona, Spain says, "Be a good sport
and smile. You're Thai, aren't you?" Clippings, a piece of pa-
per—one side *you*, the other *I*—preserved. Some say "blood
is bullshit," but there's something in my veins

and it's these letters my mother never answered. Her veins jump
out of her skin like short aerograms addressed to no one. It's a
royal romance and the heights of US presidents preserved in
envelopes tucked inside a plastic bin and stained with strong
soot. I don't know if she meant to leave them behind or not.
Thais question real motives, fictional ones come from the heart,

and when I renamed myself I thought about her heart and
whether there was room in it for me, or if there was room for
just my veins to be shoved in a pile and covered with a gaping
Thai smile. I thought about it and if the sense of Thai heritage
is so strong, then why do I have this letter from 1972 preserved

in this envelope? She preserves it so well that I can't even find
her heart anymore. I want to be strong and ask her to open
up her veins, to let me know, but Christy, it's way harder than
you make it out to be, to be Thai,

**DID YOU KNOW?** This destination features words from Dutch singer Christy Gib-
son's "About Me" page [http://www.christygibsononline.com] accessed in October
2011. The italicized phrase is by David Wagoner.

I'm having the hardest time trying to catch up. Thailand is so totally creased into these Par Avion posts, preserved. I don't know it, but I have a Thai heart and there's something climbing in my veins. *All our distance / has ended in the light.* I don't know if we're strong

at all but I try to be strong, like a Thai person would, opening up my veins in spirals to unfold sealed envelopes preserved— trying to find a heart in it

*Channel Comments (9)*

is this really Christy or just a fan? if you are really her I met you one time at temple in tampa,florida    u never took a picture with me though.

when you are alone do you speak thai or do you speak another language? you are super cool! I'm thai and can't even do what you r doing.

You are thai    anyone with a Thai heart is Thai    Most Thai people think of you as Thai

Please dont regard yourself as farang, coz you are no more farang than any of us. Being Thai is who you are not what you are. I see all the Thai-ness in you, something that millions of people who call themselves Thai lack of.

Christy, your song reminds me of bamboo mats and plastic furniture covers and the karaoke machine and how the house smelled like the metal inside a rice cooker.

Christy, your song reminds me of the basement with christmas lights and my socks on cold linoleum and falling asleep on the black pleather couch upstairs and dozing after midnight on the car ride home, four wheel drive on icy roads.

**INFORMATION:** Christy Gibson is a Dutch artist who sings traditional lookthung (Thai/Lao music from the rural northeast) and mor lam. She grew up in Korat, Thailand and is popular among Thai people, many of whom believe she sings Thai better than ethnic Thais. The author wants to question her ease of access to Thai culture and her mastery of Thai language when so many Thai people in the diaspora do not have the same access.

**DID YOU KNOW?** The first section models itself after actual comments on Christy's YouTube channel.

Christy, your song reminds me of the desire to be Thai, when I wanted it but didn't really know what it was, when it comforted me.

Christy, your voice transports me to Thailand 10 years ago, and this boi I had a crush on but never told. I have no idea what you're singing about.

Christy, my all time dream is to be your backup dancer! I look in the mirror every day and think I look very much like one of the girls from your last album. when your having auditions please email me! cuteisaangirl19@yahoo.co.th

Not sure
who this
comment is or
from, Native but
Non Native
(I also demonstrate
white desire

*Backup, Backdrop, Background*

Christy Gibson is shooting a karaoke music video at Temple of the Emerald Buddha with eight backup dancers backing up until we hit the screen, fading into Christy's background in Holland and the day, when she was six years old and she tripped, and hurt her pinky toe, but didn't tell anyone, before her family moved to Korat and how she lost her shoes between Amsterdam and BKK International because her little suitcase never made it to baggage claim.

Christy is shooting a karaoke music video at BKK baggage claim where her backup dancers come through the rubber curtain, through the carousel and around on the silver conveyor belt studded with lights.

We are each a little part of that lost suitcase, and Christy's name handwritten on the tag that failed to make it to her, and how all of her childhood in Holland was lost in that suitcase, and how in Korat she accumulated new things but did not have a container for them.

We spin around to replicate Christy's feeling of loss, stick out our right hips, turn and smile into her back.

We rise out of our own suitcases, throw them onto Christy's jet, close the hatch and walk back, replaying the video Christy's father shot of the crevice in which the Emerald Buddha actually sits, in the dark, where women selling lotus flower told Christy how cute she was

and Christy tells us how the word for cute
has the word for face
and the word for love.

Or the word for next.
Or the word for rice field.
Or the word for [something without a translation]
depending on the tone.

We dance depending on middle, high or low consonant class,
long or short vowel with no final, non-stop final or stop final
and tone mark: middle, low, high, rising, falling.

Christy says we need to be more precise or else no one will
know what we're saying.

We imagine the golden spires of the temple obscured by
Christy's sunburnt blonde head, push record, and then push
it again.

We mimic Christy's shadows interrupting a projection of
a photograph of the King set inside the crinkle of a white
hand touching and asking *how much?* drug into the vendor's
mouth framed by a hundred Beer Chang tee shirts cross-
fading into the fog machine synchronizing the movements
of our sequins neon accent the Pantene PRO-V starshow ad
pasted into the temple's floating yard line dissected by the
crisscross of flash cannon lenses and ESPN painting the dpi
between strands of Christy's hair against chedi ruins as a
backdrop at the dentist

and then Christy says, "Good."

Christy says, "I'm speaking your language."

*Stab, Suck, Scroll*

I stab the plastic top of a Thai milk tea and suck
up boba one by one, each a syllable in the song
Christy enunciates.

I match my mouth to the image. I scroll over top
the backdrop of my backup dancer body while
Christy sings.

Each tapioca is chewy and dense as Christy's
eyeballs, or her hip in a pink Western dress that
makes a YouTube user comment: I want to bump
her in Bangkok while her mouth scrolls around
the shape of a sound that has no corollary.

I chew on her face like tapioca sucked up in my
straw while I watch her scroll on a flat screen.

Every time I search 'half Thai half White,' she
haunts my cached pages.

I should be able to sound Thai no matter what.
The White part of me actually doesn't matter.
That's what you taught me, Christy.

Christy, I can totally dance better than you.

*there is a place revealed serene yet surreal*
*land of discovery beauty mystery and dignity*
*above the clouds and sun two hearts will beat as one*
*so set your spirit free be what you want to be*
*just let the sparkling seas wash all your cares away*
*more than you ever know how to be free*

Thailand is supposed to mean Land of the Free, liberty, to be liberated from slavery. Surreal to want to escape it, to want to get away from Paradise. I collect clothes with buttons and snaps for dignity's sake, as if the layers and accessories could help me become a traveler, not just look like one, although looking like one might get me a little bit closer to being free.

It's not a small step, for me it would be everything to be in a country with atmosphere, it would be surreal, like Fashion Television everyone would carry themselves with dignity. They would be White, they would be nice, they would take me away to learn about Thai silk in French, a way to gain perspective, to really understand the one thing that matters outside of myself.

It wasn't dignified but I wanted to get free of all of this. It wasn't a surreal moment when I left 113/6 for the last time. There would be many opportunities to return and I took none of them, be it destiny or fate. I told him to get away from me and he didn't, it was surreal but after all he was just one person and I was free, technically, I had more dignity than he could ever scrape off the ground, I had more dignity than the dirt living in his eyes.

**DID YOU KNOW?** This travel package features lyrics to the song in the Tourism Authority of Thailand commercial "Once in a Lifetime."

I thought I would be famous, I was obsessed with French cinema, I kept telling myself I was free until I stopped thinking about it, until I was away for 20, 30, 40 years and realized I was the one chained by my guts to a childhood memory I called surreal.

Inhabiting that surreal architecture, I dressed up in all the dignity I could wash and iron. I said, *I'm the only one who'll be so far away and never free.*

# THE AMERICAN MUSEUM OF
# THAI NATIONAL CHARACTER

*It would look like Siam, but like Siam as seen
through the eyes of an American artist.*

- Richard Rodgers

**INFORMATION:** "...Even though our view of Siam couldn't be completely authentic, Oscar and I were determined to depict the Orientals in the story as characters, not caricatures, which has all too often been the case in the musical theatre. Our aim was to portray the king and his court with humanity and believability, while avoiding the disease Oscar used to call 'research poison'" [*Music from the musical The King and I* CD liner notes, citing Richard Rodgers' *Musical Stages*].

## PAD THAI (1990 -    )

In The American Museum of Thai National Character, Rirkrit Tiravanija (pronounced Tea-rah-vah-nit) empties everything out except himself and an electric wok. In this duration piece, which builds on years of expertise as a cultural worker and chef, Tea-rah-vah-nit will make Pad Thai twenty-four hours a day for a period of six months.

Museum members on their obligatory stroll toss half-eaten bowls in the bins, curiosity satisfied, before discussing the exhibit's merits over cocktails at the ritzy Thai restaurant across the street. On First Tuesdays, free admission draws broke art students and the homeless for a quick cruise-n-schmooze and a free meal. Plastic forks and wooden chopsticks pile up. Tea-rah-vah-nit's installation of overflowing black garbage bins is like a karaoke ghost-sculpture—disconcerting, thrilling, simple.

The administration and curatorial staff were reluctant to turn the gallery into a soup kitchen. But the piles of rotting Pad Thai (as well as the flies and mold growth that accumulate) is a fresh commentary on the popularity of this quintessential Thai dish within a system of modernity spiraling toward entropy. Despite bugs, mice and mice turds, the red pepper flakes and hardened rice sticks are still Thai.

This exhibit is about the perseverance of the Thai spirit.

Everyone wants to watch the Pad Thai rot.

**INFORMATION:** Some language is pulled from Jerry Saltz's article "Conspicuous Consumption" on Rirkrit Tiravanija's installations, published in *New York Magazine* on May 7, 2007.

## TAKE YOUR ORDER (2010 -    )

In The American Museum of Thai National Character, there is an exhibit of current menus from every single Thai restaurant in America. The Artist wheat-pastes the menus to the walls, floor to ceiling, menus on top of menus. On Sunday afternoons, The Artist attempts to remove the menus, uncovering the original wall surface as much as possible.

Then The Artist begins to wheat-paste again.

## KEEP WARM (1980 -    )

In The American Museum of Thai National Character, there is
an exhibit of abandoned rice cookers rescued from thrift stores.
Most are broken and missing parts; others are brand new and
never used. The Artist plugs them in one at a time. The Artist
then stacks the ones that work together and the ones that
don't work together, evoking the resilience of the Thai people.

## AMAZING (1998 -    )

In The American Museum of Thai National Character, there is an exhibit of popular adjectives White tourists have used, historically, to describe Thailand. The words are pieced together using wooden alphabet blocks. Museum-goers can barely walk through these rooms, which is a testament to the buoyancy of the Thai spirit.

**REJECTION (1960 -    )**

In The American Museum of Thai National Character, there is an exhibit of rejection letters addressed to Thai women who applied to secretarial colleges in the UK in the 1960s. Each envelope has been neatly opened by a letter-opener. They are dropped one by one at one-minute intervals from the ceiling via a mechanized arm, creating a growing pile on the gallery floor. The shear amount of these letters is a testament to the persistence of the Thai spirit.

Some of the letters fall out of their envelopes and unfold.

## CUSTOMS (1970 -    )

In The American Museum of Thai National Character, there is an exhibit of luggage that was previously lost on Thai-US flights, confiscated by customs and never claimed. The Artists wheel the luggage into the gallery and arrange them in sculptural forms. Some of the lighter bags are flung on top. Then The Artists dismantle the luggage sculptures and wheel them away in carts before the entire performance is repeated. The content of each luggage maintains itself as a mystery, symbolizing the enigmatic nature of the Thai spirit.

**4,633 (1944 -    )**

In The American Museum of Thai National Character, there is an exhibit of 4,633 monitors. Each monitor represents the number of times Yul Brynner performed the role of THE KING in THE KING AND I during his lifetime. Each monitor plays a different video on loop. Each video shows The Artist reading a different line of Yul's from the play. The resulting chaotic audio-visual overlap symbolizes the frenetic pace of contemporary Thai life.

**BANNED (1974 -    )**

In The American Museum of Thai National Character, there is an ongoing screening of American films about Thailand that have been banned in Thailand.

Films and show dates are as follows:

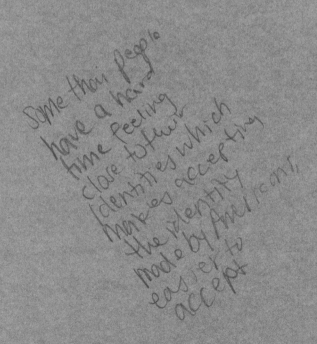

Some thai people have a hard time feeling close to fun identities which makes accepting the identity made by Americans easier to accept

# THE ROMANCE OF THE SIAMESE DREAM

*Because no matter what story I tell them...*
*writers invent things about me, and once*
*they've invented them they believe them.*

- Yul Brynner,
*Yul: The Man Who Would Be King*

# THE ROMANCE OF THE SIAMESE DREAM

## Overture

*In a world between reality and imagination,*
*a woman creates a fiction to cover up her past*
*and a man creates a character that will forever change*
*his future.*

*Will they become who they are meant to be?*
*Only the romance of the dream will tell.*

## Act One

YUL BRYNNER is having one of his recurring dreams.

He's on stage for the 4,634[th] performance of THE KING AND I.

The theatre is deserted. All the work lights and house lights are on.

It's hot.

A traveling spotlight is trained on him.

YUL paces, barefoot, to the proscenium. The spotlight follows.

**HIGHLIGHTS:** Yul Brynner performed the role of the King in *The King and I* approximately 4,633 times during the course of his lifetime. He was known to make up stuff about his life in interviews, like saying he was descended from Genghis Khan. The real Anna Leonowens was born in Bombay in working class military camps; her mother was most likely mixed race (half South Asian, half White). At some point in her life Anna decided to rewrite her past and told people she was born in England and was an upper class Englishwoman. Everyone believed her—even her grandchildren. The author is intrigued by the way these two people reinvented their lives, and how the characters they brought to life are wrapped up in *The King and I* saga.

**DID YOU KNOW?** This piece was written while listening to the Smashing Pumpkins' *Siamese Dream* (1993) album.

YUL paces, barefoot, to the scrim. The spotlight follows.

YUL paces, barefoot, to the wing stage right. The spotlight doesn't follow.

Thinking he's free of it, YUL turns his back on the spot, which immediately makes a beeline for him.

YUL swears he can hear the light chuckle.

A large rice cooker appears stage center. Its top is open. It is clean and empty. The electric cord spills out of its side. The metal is buzzing.

In the dream the rice cooker tells YUL its name is TIGER.

YUL paces up to TIGER, barefoot, exposes his chest, raises his brow, points his finger.

TIGER (telepathically): Wow, I'm so not impressed.

YUL (emphatically): Go on go on go on!

TIGER (telepathically): OK, so...I'm a wormhole. I didn't show up last time you had this dream, so if I were you, I'd take a ride.

YUL can feel TIGER's hot breath.

TIGER wants YUL to come inside.

YUL gingerly inserts his bald head into the cooker. He sheds his silk jacket, his silk fisherman pants, and his two gold anklets.

## Act Two

YUL emerges out on the other side. He's on stage again. The house lights and work lights are out. All the spots are focused on him, blinding white. He's sitting on the floor, knees drawn up to his chin, naked and hairless.

TIGER is gone. In TIGER's place is ANNA. The REAL ANNA Leonowens from THE KING AND I. ANNA is wearing a giant hoop skirt that fills two-thirds of the stage. She's wearing a strange brooch set with two tiger claws. She's here to teach YUL the art of acting.

ANNA (dismissively): What a child you are.

YUL (defensively): I used to be a boy. What I choose is my choice.

ANNA (excitedly): Do you want to pretend? Do you want to play a game of make-believe?

Backstage the dressing rooms are filled with white underwear and metal forks, all in disarray. ANNA directs YUL to go clean it up.

YUL is sweating. He can't stack up all the forks perfectly, they keep slipping and falling. When YUL folds one pair of underwear, three more appear.

ANNA (inquisitively): Do you want to change your name?

YUL (decisively): People don't know my real self, and they're not about to find out!

At the proscenium appears a railing. ANNA and YUL lean on it and look out into the audience.

ANNA (reminiscing): I came to America from the same port as the Titanic. And I...

YUL (with gusto, completing ANNA's sentence):...and I am the King of Siam!

YUL feels slightly ridiculous, like he's in a blockbuster movie.

ANNA (in the manner of good advice): Reinvent yourself the moment you disembark.

## Act Three

ANNA directs YUL to stop organizing the underwear and forks backstage and make a living poem out of it.

Instead, YUL writes a dead letter to ANNA's grandmother.

YUL (poetically):

> Dear Sleeping Dictionary,
> Won't you wake?
> I need to look up the word, "Character."
> Army, British Bombay. Where is
> The Company?
> Uncle Tom,
> Cousin Tom,
> Husband Tom,
> Sleeping Tom.
> Penang, Prince of Wales.

The stage turns into a raft on the river, secured to the shore by ropes and chains.

ANNA (nostalgically): I wrote my biography in eight pages. My grandchildren believed every word of it. All it requires is that you act the part.

YUL (apprehensively): So, I pretend to be someone I want to be...

ANNA (definitively): ...and I finally become that person, or she becomes me.

### Finale (Ultimo)

ANNA stares at YUL with entire singleness of eye. In thirty seconds YUL grows a full head of hair that keeps growing down to the floor, across the stage, into the aisles. In thirty seconds ANNA has progressed to old age and is going blind. Her dark, deep-set eyes turn into balls of hard white wax.

**Starring** LEONARDO DICAPRIO and CLAIRE DANES
**Also Starring** RAPTOR

Leonardo diCaprio runs down a white sand beach at an international seaside resort, looking for controversy.

Everything that's banned in Thailand goes to live on THE WHITE BEACH. It's a parallel universe.

It's always August 1994 on THE WHITE BEACH.

Part of THE WHITE BEACH is in Thailand, where Joni Anwar and Louis Scott become the youngest pop singers ever. They name themselves RAPTOR after the two dinosaurs in the kitchen at the end of JURASSIC PARK, and also because it sounds like "rapper," which is cool.

The other part of THE WHITE BEACH is in Pittsburgh on the set of MY SO-CALLED LIFE. 15-year-old Wilson Cruz is Puerto Rican *and* gay. Wilson Cruz doesn't have anything, but 15-year-old Claire Danes is going to win because she's White.

Leonardo diCaprio has come to spring Claire Danes from one of the number of fine rustic restaurants that have permanently dropped anchor in the sheltered cove, THE BROKEDOWN

**HIGHLIGHTS:** This exotic adventure sequence is a mash-up of deleted scenes from *The Beach* (2000) (starring Leonardo) and *Brokedown Palace* (1999) (starring Claire), cut with language from a Tourist Organization of Thailand travel brochure for Pattaya circa the late 1960s or early 1970s, printed by Far East Press Co., Ltd., Bangkok.

PALACE RESTAURANT, where she's been a server for 33 years. Despite being based on Thailand, the restaurant is actually in Manila.

Claire Danes told *Premiere* magazine that Manila QUOTE smelled of cockroaches, with rats all over, and that there is no sewage system, and the people do not have anything—no arms, no legs, no eyes.

Leonardo diCaprio is bulldozing the natural beach setting to make it more "paradise-like."

Leonardo diCaprio practices running back and forth on the beach for an hour and a half, then breaks for lunch at THE BROKEDOWN. Inside, RAPTOR is shooting their new karaoke music video.

In the video everyone has hair like Jordan Catalano. Joni Anwar and Louis Scott throw paper airplanes in oversize flannel button-downs. They make awkward glances at each other in the lockered hallway and look longingly at empty plastic desks in slow motion.

RAPTOR is in the kitchen with Claire Danes, reenacting a scene from JURASSIC PARK and rapping. Tonight they're going to play a comeback concert at the JURASSIC PARK RED BULL 18-HOLE GOLF COURSE ISLAND.

**DID YOU KNOW?** The Thai pop band Raptor formed in 1994, around the same time that *My So-Called Life* went on the air in the US. Claire Danes really told Premiere Magazine that stuff about Manila (Wikipedia).

The next scene catches everyone's fancy.

Claire Danes is holding hands with a young Thai woman named Pinky.

In her other hand Claire Danes is holding a snorkel from the hotel. In Pinky's other hand are two fish trawled by an original fishing villager. These are the new featured activities.

Claire Danes and Pinky walk up from the bioluminescent plankton to the white sand beach, invigorated in 70s style bikinis, in front of the 18-hole golf course and all the dead coral.

It's a photo shoot for a Tourism Authority of Thailand brochure that aims to sell:

a state of mind.

# THE WHITE ELEPHANT RIDE

**Starring** TONY JAA, RUN-RUN/JIG-JIG, DEKE WEAVER and MAYA as Buddha's Mother

**Brought to you by** BEER CHANG, The Elephant Beer

Tony Jaa wants to go where he can't be found.

Tony Jaa runs into Maya's dream the night before she gives birth to the Buddha.

In Maya's dream Tony Jaa is The King of the White Elephant.

In Maya's dream Tony Jaa is a commercial for Beer Chang.

In Maya's dream Tony Jaa is the remake of *The King of the White Elephant* sponsored by Beer Chang.

In Maya's dream Tony Jaa is at the train station.

**HIGHLIGHTS:** This adventure jungle tour zips through Ernest Hemingway's short story *Hills Like White Elephants* (1927) [said to be about a couple dealing with abortion, though it is never directly discussed; "I'm looking for a gift and a curse" and "Could we try it?" are lines from the story], Tony Jaa's nonstop carnage in the movie *The Protector* (2005) [in which he kicks major ass in order to save his baby elephant], Sid Fleischman's children's book *The White Elephant* (Green Willow Books, 2006) [Run-Run/Jig-Jig is an amalgamation of Fleischman's main character Run-Run and Hemingway's Jig], and Deke Weaver's *Elephant* performance [http://unreliablebestiary.org/elephant.php] as reviewed by Marissa Perel in *"Elephant," or Why I Love Performance Art* on Art21 Blog, December 9, 2010 [http://blog.art21.org/2010/12/09/elephant-or-why-i-love-performance-art/] and Maya's dream the night before she gave birth to the Buddha.

**INFORMATION:** This tour was written while listening to Ladytron's *Gravity the Seducer* (2011) album, which opens with the song "White Elephant." The form is loosely inspired by Ronaldo V. Wilson's "Dream in a Fair" in *Poems of the Black Object* (Futurepoem Books, 2009) and his advice to "seek the fog."

**DID YOU KNOW?** The word "white" is used 54 times in this tour.

Run-Run/Jig-Jig says the hills look like white elephants.

They are drinking coconut water out of shot glasses. Tony Jaa is not paying attention.

"I'm looking for a gift and a curse."

"Could we try it?"

Run-Run/Jig-Jig is holding Tiger's eyes in hir palms. They are wet and cold white eggs.

*When I close my eyes, I'm being chased by a Tiger. I want to go where I can't be found.*

In Maya's dream she's drinking a jug of white milk. She's lactose intolerant.

The white milk becomes a huge lake that freezes into white ice.

Maya is on a white iceberg in the white lake.

She's visited by a white tiger with crossed eyes, a Siamese cat with crossed eyes, and a white elephant.

It's snowing.

The white tiger offers her its eyes.

The Siamese cat offers her its eyes.

The white elephant offers her an Xmas card with a lotus flower on the front.

Maya takes the lotus flower Xmas card.

The four eyes drop to the snowy bank, affixed to crystals of ice.

She's an iceberg.

She wakes up.

*All I want is white.*

Tony Jaa runs out onto the platform. The train is nowhere in sight.

Deke Weaver is at a white church dressed as a little old white lady from Elkton, South Dakota.

Deke Weaver is setting up the white elephant sale and the white elephant gift exchange.

Deke Weaver has a stack of Xmas cards with white elephants on them.

Run-Run/Jig-Jig and Tony Jaa find an iceberg.

*Here's where we can't be found. Here's where all the lost things are.*

They omit. Inside are all the white elephants that can't escape.

Maya, Run-Run/Jig-Jig, Tony Jaa and Deke Weaver are at the white elephant gift exchange in the white church.

They sit in a white circle on white lawn chairs.

Run-Run/Jig-Jig has two Tiger's eyes.

Maya has a stack of Xmas cards with white elephants on them.

Tony Jaa has *The King of the White Elephant* on DVD.

Deke Weaver just picked a Beer Chang t-shirt, but he wants to steal.

No one is ready to give up.

In Maya's dream everything is white.

Run-Run/Jig-Jig, Maya, Tony Jaa and Deke Weaver go on a white elephant ride through the white fog around the white iceberg walking in her white sleep.

They stop and drink white tea with white half and half and the white steam rising up.

It starts to white snow.

Run-Run/Jig-Jig looks at the whites of Tony Jaa's eyes, which are actually pink.

Maya opens one of the cards and begins to write. *Wishing you all the white...*

Tony Jaa tosses the DVD case to the floor.

Maya wakes up.

There's a white elephant in the room!

*I want it. I want what I lost.*

Maya omits the iceberg from her dream.

Run-Run/Jig-Jig, Tony Jaa, Deke Weaver and all the white elephants in it.

Maya gives birth to all the white.

White milk, white ice, white snow, white elephants, white tourists, white rice, white tigers, white Siamese cats with crossed eyes.

They all grow darker in the cold.

Run-Run/Jig-Jig squeezes the Tiger's eyes in hir fists until they burst.

*I've crossed them. Now I can't be found.*

*I'm in love with Tony Jaa, but I don't want to have his white elephant.*

*When I close my eyes, all I see are white elephants. Inside me, something omits.*

Run-Run/Jig-Jig runs out to the platform. The train has just left the station.

Run-Run/Jig-Jig stares at the hills of alleged white elephant projects through the white smoke.

Tony Jaa is looking for a gift and a curse.

The white elephant wants to go where it can't be found.

# THE FLOATING MARKET

It is difficult to find adjectives to describe the floating market economy where everything comes to you—where everything is potentially within reach if only you daydream long enough—in the Buddhist way and let your mind float on water—a tireless promoter of floating Jim Thompson discovered silk weavers floating outside his home—what an opportunity to make a floating market of silk—one of the world's most colorful and unusual activities—colorful and unusual being the adjectives used to describe—one of the must-see White men who transformed Thailand and never left—in the Jim Thompson House gift shop Michael Shaowanasai dances in yellow silk pumps made out of Jim Thompson silk and scarves with fake headlines—the visitor can look into each home—happy brown-skinned children splash and swim like porpoises discovered outside Jim's window—he harvests silk from the porpoises who weave the silk for him to sell to the floating market in Milan—high fashion markets are floating for a chance at this high quality material—they'll pay any price—daydreaming about European women in Thai silk and Thai women in European silk floating like porpoises on the river—take a look into each home and watch the porpoises play—look how happy they are to have nothing—no arms, no legs, no eyes—

Jim Thompson took an afternoon walk in the jungle of Malaysia in 1967 and never returned—he's floating somewhere haunting the property—the alley dogs bark in the middle of the night—maybe it was a man-eating tiger—maybe he was

**HIGHLIGHTS:** Some language is taken from a Tourist Organization of Thailand travel brochure for The Floating Market circa the late 1960s or early 1970s, printed by Pra Cha Chang & Co., Ltd., Bangkok. This destination references the Jodie Foster and Chow Yun-Fat remake, *Anna and the King* (1999).

**DID YOU KNOW?** The author visited the Jim Thompson House in 2011; one of its exhibits showcased a short film by Michael Shaowanasai, title unknown, which is referenced in this piece.

run over by a truck driver—the King of Thai Silk floating now in the market he created—in the worldwide popularity of Thai silk—everyone smiles and waves as he passes by—water-gypsy farmers come to haggle—woven into legend Jim Thompson floats above the market with everything—a top 25 tourist attraction open everyday—Silk King disappeared—sister murdered shortly after—his involvement in the OSS—reasons for his floating—his daydreaming walk in the jungle where he disappeared—the number of times "jungle" is used to describe an unknown threat—although it is difficult to find adjectives he outfitted an entire production of THE KING AND I—Jodie Foster and Chow Yun-Fat are in the jungle in Malaysia filming yet another remake—they find that Jim is still alive—floating in a canal and living with silk-weaving porpoises who abducted him—as they float by they watch the porpoises weaving on their looms—souvenir stores and several restaurants—the porpoises are shaded by strange shaped colorful umbrellas—the porpoises are attracting buyers—they attracted Jim and he was high from the daydream so much that he fell in love and decided to stay—the porpoises smile (as everyone does) to Jodie Foster and Chow Yun-Fat—Jim shows his blackened teeth—the mild narcotic that kept him floating—in his daydream the porpoises turn into beautiful women weaving silk from finely spun strands of Jim's flesh—when Jodie Foster and Chow Yun-Fat find him he has no arms, no legs, no eyes—

he's smiling—as everyone does in Thailand—even though he's in Malaysia—the porpoises are CIA operatives on a top secret mission to abduct the King of Thai Silk and protect him from communist snipers in the jungle—Jodie and Chow want to bring him back to Thailand—with the discovery of Jim Thompson in their hands the ban on ANNA AND THE KING could be floated—the added dividend—water police

negotiate with porpoises—the crush is terrific—the famed
Floating Market Tour now has a new stop—Jim Thompson—a
blind smiling torso ornamented in silk woven by CIA porpoises
in Malaysia in the style of THE KING who never left—

Jim Thompson is alive—a well dressed ghost splashing in the
khlong with the other porpoises—ready to float the ban and
discover the America that floats through Thailand—

none of the traditional charm sacrificed—

# THE KING AND I...I

Christy Gibson is directing a new karaoke musical remake of THE KING AND I. Set in 1985, the production commemorates the death of exotic leading man and Famous Fictional Thai Person, Yul Brynner, and will serve as a promotional video brochure for the Tourism Authority of Thailand (TAT).

Christy casts Pete Burns as Anna, based on his aesthetic choices in Dead or Alive's iconic music video for YOU SPIN ME ROUND (LIKE A RECORD PLAYER). Christy feels that he is of a kindred artistic vision.

*Well I...I set my sights on you (and no one else will do)*
*And I...I've got to have my way now baby*
*As soon as I (I! I! I!) saw the word Thailand*
*Well I (I! I! I!) just knew it was my destiny (oh destiny)*

This is Pete's version of Deborah Kerr's version of Margaret Landon's version of Anna Leonowens' love song for Siam. It also doubles as Pete's version of Yul Brynner's version of The Siamese King. It is a testament to the mutability of Thai character.

*And I I I I!*

Yul Brynner and Jim Thompson fight over the role of THE KING. Naturally, Brynner's long-standing position in this role, ranging from musical theatre to television and film, means he's mastered all nuance and deeply understands the plight of the character. However, Thompson's reputation as THE SILK KING and as a tourist attraction clearly pulls its own weight.

Ultimately, the number of times Yul Brynner opens his silk jacket to reveal his bare chest is a winner for Pete Burns.

Pete Burns spins around and says, "Only *male* elephants, your majesty?"

The dramatic turning point of the musical is an interpretation of Leonardo diCaprio's THE BEACH using a cast made up entirely of white elephant puppets. It will be called THE WHITE BEACH, a Siamese version of the famous American book. When the puppets talk, apostrophes fall out of their stitched mouths.

Some of Christy's cultural mastery is rubbing off on Pete, who's perfecting Christy's look. Pete ushers the sophistication of 1862 Deborah Kerr into 1985. The little royal children hide in Pete's hair as well as Pete's hoop skirt.

Christy decides to emphasize Anna's geography lesson. Growing up in Holland, Ice and Snow are things deeply close to Christy's heart. Believing in snow can save your life.

Pete Burns spins around and says, "Oh, The White Is Siam."

# SIAMESE WHITE

*Well I...I set my sights on you*
*(and no one else will do)*
*And I...I've got to have my way now*
*baby...I I I I...I got to be your friend*
*And I I I I...would like to move in*
*just a little bit closer (a little bit closer)*

Christy Gibson casts Pete Burns as Anna Leonowens in order to move closer to the essence of THE KING AND I. Her lookthung rewrite of "Getting to Know You" threatens to become a big hit. Classic remakes are in and Christy wants to capture Siam through the eyes of whoever will do the best job of seeing Siam from the inside.

Not a strange man, but her very close friend Pete Burns brings gay fabulousity to the role that could potentially fling the play into the now, which is what Christy wants, a brochure-sized re-telling, now that she's an ambassador for the rich diversity of the TAT licensed tours program and closer to the pulse of the Thai people—a bit comical but a good friend of THE KING.

She asks Pete to swing his hips more. "You could really take the spotlight away from Yul Brynner," and he does, even with just one eye. The viewers are trans-fixed 54 seconds in to the commercial. Overcome with the paralyzing desire to experience Amazing Thailand, in less than 24 hours they've already booked their Grand Palace/Long Neck/Monkey tour. The "NOW" is a powerful moment in which to harness the imagination of the West, and that's just what they do.

Creepy golden fingernails punctuate the space behind Pete as he spins closer and closer to Yul, his silk jacket opening to expose his bare chest for the billionth time. You can't take your eyes off them—your eyes are gone.

Pete plays Anna extra friendly, which works to his advantage. Pete teaches his friends the royal children and his majesty's mistresses his version of *Home Sweet Home* in just 28 seconds. The chanting of the pseudo-Oriental theme should oppose you as it fills the background, tinkling nasal and attractive now that we've heard it from Pete Burns' lips.

He brings us closer to the contrasts between Eastern and Western cultures, longingly attracting us, which they do, and longingly attracting us to Pete's Anna. The TAT asked Christy to do "Western People Funny," happy people in White face, *friend-ly, friend-li-er, friend-li-est*, which will bring Pete closer to his destiny of simple Eurasian fusion.

In foreign country it is best to like everyone until you leave. Now leave! Yul calls Pete "Sir," as modern and scientific as you can get. You'd better go do your homework now. After the friendship bridge tour White people are in, closer than ever.

*As a teacher I've been learning, you'll forgive me if I boast.
And I've now become an expert on the subject I like most.
Getting to know you, getting to know all about you. Getting
to like you, getting to hope you like me. Putting it my way
but nicely, you are precisely my cup of tea. Getting to feel
free and easy. When I am with you, getting to know what to
say. Haven't you noticed, suddenly I'm bright and breezy?
Because of all the beautiful and new things I'm learning
about you, day by day.*

Pete Burns wants to be a lowly toad for Yul Brynner today, but
all of the Siamese people are toads so it's nothing special.
Christy is an expert on this and the Siamese trust her. Christy
says, Yul might pay more attention if you carry a whip. *Me?
A whip?* says Pete, coyly. Playing Anna isn't as easy as he
thought, but it's turning out to be so much fun, sipping Thai
ice tea every afternoon at the market out of a plastic bag.

Pete wants to tell Yul about tea-bagging and works on a proper
translation all day and slips it under Yul's secret chamber
door, maintaining an easy level of fantasy appropriate for the
character. He's becoming an expert at perfecting the image of
a White woman through White eyes. "It could have been me,"
Pete says, "on that boat in 1862. If I were there I would say
to Anna Leonowens, Follow your heart. You should have left,
say, when you had the chance, because now we drink imported
tea and many people have played your character trying to find
the essence. Me, I just imagine Yul Brynner opening his silk
jacket to reveal his bare chest everyday and it gets me going.
I think now I am an expert on her character and could teach a
thing or two to Irene, Gertrude, Deborah, Jodie—easy.

**DID YOU KNOW?** This destination features lyrics to "Getting to Know You" from
the musical *The King And I*.

"Yul's not a stranger, usually a very good friend. Dancing with him is really easy, I just let him lead. I let him forget the AND...I say, *and...and...and I*. Yes your majesty, your mastery must be expert. I wait for him to bring his hand around my waist and draw me close like a teacup. The rehearsal for that scene lasted all day and into the night. I'm a very difficult woman, but me, I'm a more difficult man, generally, so I'm glad Christy gave me this role, this chance of a lifetime, it's not easy but I'm excited for the fireworks between me and Yul the next day we shoot. I hope it's my fault that Prince Chulalongkorn says, Rise, rise up like soldiers, no eye to no eye. Tea and teaching, these are Anna's legacies, of which we are by now experts."


"Christy, an expert on me, fixes tea, makes it easy to say I am what I make believe I am, today."

# EXOTIC LEADING MAN

*His name, we were told, was Yul Brynner, which meant nothing to us. He scowled in our direction, sat down on the stage and crossed his legs, tailor-fashion, then plunked one whacking chord on his guitar and began to howl in a strange language that no one could understand. He looked savage, he sounded savage, and there was no denying that he projected a feeling of controlled ferocity. [...] We had our king.*

Yul Brynner will not be usurped from his role as THE KING no matter how often Jim Thompson's ghost will sit in his dressing room and scowl. Christy Gibson is counting on Pete Burns to steal the show from him, using not ferocity but homoeroticism in a sub-textual language Yul won't get, busy whacking the air with his Siamese no-arms and Siamese no-eyes, savage in the ways Pete will be sensual, throwing Yul off-kilter in a strange balletic advertisement for the TAT.

Christy will play Anna's strange confidant Lady Thiang, head wife to THE KING. Her rendition of "Western People Funny" includes a yoo-hoo nod to savage Holland. That's why she whistles instead of scowls. She's as brave as she can make believe she is in mastering this art form, a whack in the face of the *et cethera, et cethera, et cethera* ferocity of Yul Brynner, who points at the sky streaked with White with a ferocity that threatens to be overshadowed by Christy's bravery and Pete's hips, strange truths as Yul is now too old to polka about as he once could, whacking the floor.

**DID YOU KNOW?** This destination features a quote regarding the moment Rodgers and Hammerstein met Brynner in a casting call for *The King and I*, as quoted in *Music from the musical The King and I* CD liner notes, which originally appeared in Richard Rodgers' *Musical Stages*. *The Love of Siam* (2007) is a Thai movie starring Mario Maurer.

The Love of Siam is unrequited and there is no kissing involved. When THE KING looks at Pete, what does he see with his no-eye? Christy scowls. "Be careful with gags. Don't tread on any savage toes with your no-legs. Don't tread on any savage scuttling toads bowing before Yul Brynner with a ferocity that was learned in rehearsal." When Pete Burns scowls, it's rather sexy. "You were just that little strange white spot to me before I took my TEFL course which THE KING required." The better of two being neither, Yul is ready to whack his slaves in front of Pete, who rather enjoys that sort of whacking in the presence of his lord and master. Not savage but something called sado-masochism.

THE KING tries very hard to understand, etc etc but ferocity proves to open more doors. Christy explains that English words are all we speak, with strange accents like silk flags and ribbon. "You're the subject I like most," Yul scowls, a scowl that says "I'm putting it my way but nicely," *whack whack-whack*. His strange cranium slants with such savage ferocity that he can't be anything but KING.

# MANIFEST DESTINY TOUR

Christy Gibson and Pete Burns host Thailand's new travel television show, *Manifest Destiny,* sponsored by 7Eleven. Such a glittering duo is destined for gay disco. To raise funds for the pilot they launch the *Manifest Destiny Tour*—in every city they cook one dish from *The Yul Brynner Cookbook* and once every dish is made they'll have reached their goal.

In the spa at the hotel, *Globe Trekker's* Ian Wright offers them a lifetime's worth of advice: "Having an accent helps," and "Don't eat everything, even if Lifetime Network tells you to." The show is quickly picked up in the States; they manifest an audience of bored suburban Whites within milliseconds.

Christy and Pete's first stop is a generic temple ruin at sunset, a very authentic backdrop to the destiny of the crumbling and stubborn Thais. Making eye contact with Pete, Ian says, "Once you get over the annual monkey festival, you understand the meaning of 'look but don't touch.'"

They meet more tourists than actual hill tribes, and the added feature of Oriental pomp makes the tour sweet, less acidic than the States. Even with Ian's help, Christy and Pete have a lifetime of chances they're willing to take. Pete predictably bites through a chili once and runs around searching for sugar, wisely leaving it to the manifesto of a professional like Ian.

Christy and Pete's second stop is the airport terminal of Destiny Awaits Airlines, a spin-off, where passengers have to pay for blankets on the frigid flight. In his charming accent Ian haggles with Thai women, living up to their expectations. His personality takes up two streets and makes a disturbing impact.

The tour ends in a tuk-tuk where they meet Kathy Lee, Yul Brynner's 24-year-old 4th wife, whose destiny was crushed when 65-year-old Yul died in 1985, just 2 years after their marriage, leaving his lifetime achievement, an award-winning cookbook. Kathy took the opportunity to manifest her future.

For a poor Malaysian ballerina who played the part of a dancing girl in THE KING AND I, appearing once on "Manifest Destiny" made her even more famous, at once. "I can get all the ingredients back home," Kathy Lee says. "In a time when you can get Thailand on Amazon it's amazing to have the real manifestation of a country."

At two of the most accessible destinations on their touring schedule, Ian tries to avoid Pete's lethal sting. One night in Bangkok proves to be a lifetime of golf in a museum of lesser known casualties, destination and cheap entertainment. Everyone has a personal story about Thailand, but not everyone has a destiny on a nearby island, or a stunning 150-foot reclining shopping mall.

"Once you start eating, it's quite difficult to stop," says Ian in the episode "A Lifetime of Food Fit For The King And You." In Krabi Pete Burns develops a crush on the White Cave Man who's fighting against mass tourism destroying The Blue Lagoon. A fine and fascinating tale takes just moments to manifest:

Christy Gibson and Pete Burns' *Manifest Destiny Travel Television Tour* Happens Just Once In a Lifetime And Occupies Our Dreams Forever.

# THE SILK KING AND I

Infuriated over not being cast as THE KING in Christy Gibson's karaoke musical remake of THE KING AND I, Jim Thompson is rallying independent cinema to produce the low-budget THE SILK KING AND I.

"I've always wanted my own musical," says Jim. "The details of my disappearance and death have been the subject of much debate and controversy and even a Choose Your Own Adventure book. I'm confident I can write a compelling story, and this is my chance to share it with the world. I was saved by Thai people. Just because I'm a ghost doesn't mean I can't act."

Jim casts me as ANNA. I jump at the chance to show my love for Thailand, and for very little pay. That's how much this country means to me.

The plot includes CIA mafia meetings inside temples, ferry-boat chases down canals, tuk-tuk chases, tiger attacks and jungle snipers, as per usual.

The whole musical is meant to occur in The Floating Market on boats. Set designers scramble to redress corporate advertising and White people to restore Bangkok to the authentic serenity of 1967. Jim conducts rehearsals over Skype. Since he's a ghost it's hard for me to figure out what he wants from my performance, but I'm trying my best, which is all that matters.

**DID YOU KNOW?** Jim Thompson really has a choose-your-own-adventure book [Gilligan, Shannon. *The Case of the Silk King. Choose Your Own Adventure #14.* Chooseco. Waitsfield, Vermont, 1986, 2005].

I happen to be an expert at teaching English as a foreign, secondary, or other language. My approach is always the same: I begin by getting to know where my students are at. I'm consistent.

I could have been an excellent governess in 1862, perhaps even better than ANNA herself. My tweets from inside the harem would have leaked despite THE KING's firewalls, and gone viral on Facebook. With dial-up you can only do so much, but if there's the potential to reach just one person, it's worth it. I'm patient.

The relationship between Jim and I is crucial. He works on making his ghostly appearance bare more weight to balance my gung-ho fearlessness. I deliver my lines to a green screen and Jim is Photoshopped in. He feels inadequate.

Yul Brynner caves and decides to coach Jim for the role. "You don't owe me anything," Yul says, "I just want to help." His connection to the story and the role of THE KING is so deep, he volunteers to round out Jim's approach and give it more flavor.

Today Yul teaches Jim how to embody the word, "tycoon."

# DELETED SCENES

*It's alright. I can imagine the rest.*

- Leonardo diCaprio,
deleted scene from *The Beach*

# DELETED SCENE

## FLEXISTYLY

When I Google "paradise" I find Tilda Swinton on Ko Phi Phi
leading a commune of stoned travelers, tampons, triple A
  batteries
and White people who don't take shits.

In a video installation Tilda stands in front of an SLR camera
backed with tinsel. Tilda performs in silence as Orlando,
changing sex in the afternoon, and once again before breakfast.
When the tinsel shimmers, sie / s/he / ze shimmers more, like
  Shimizu.

Everyone wants to make the moment last forever,
but it's a stop motion picture. They make a subtle shift and
  snap.
Moby plays, and so they repeat. Each minute is different—
not flexisexuality or Angelina Jolie in *Foxfire* or FlexiStyle,
but Virginia's Vita—


                              a flexistyly that shutters and pops.


**HIGHLIGHTS:** Many of these Deleted Scenes were written in an online collabora-
tive writing experiment instigated by Yael Villafranca in January 2012.

**DID YOU KNOW?** "In a tropical ginger from China, some individuals are male in
the morning, making pollen, while others are female in the morning, receiving
pollen. They switch sexes in the afternoon. This phenomenon, called flexistyly, is
known in eleven families of flowering plants. The ginger's diurnal sex change is
not too different from how hamlets mate, where members of a mating pair switch
back and forth between male and female once a minute." —Joan Roughgarden,
*Evolution's Rainbow* (University of California Press, 2004).

**INFORMATION:** This scene references Tilda Swinton in *The Beach* as well as
*Orlando* (1992) [http://www.youtube.com/watch?v=fw6SxyoIxQc].

## WIDE SHOT

In a country without barriers I make some reservations with Anthony Bourdain. I pretend I'm his sidekick and pride my-self on delivering the wittiest lines to get cut. Bourdain is non-impressed and looks out a wooden window toward what-ever he's eating, an octogenarian tranny and hard nipples. Thai people sit in plastic chairs behind him eating the same cheap noodles. They're not happening, they're whatever, and with some reservation I drag them further into frame.

*As an exhausted silence settles over the table, well into my cups, I\'ll look straight at camera and sarcastically say, in my most unctuous, television \"host-sums-up\" voice, \" So.... What have we learned today?\" This is a cue to producer and shooters that I\'m fucking DONE. That it\'s time to \"get some wides\", meaning, the crew steps way back and shoots some generic \"wide shots\" from a distance.*

**DID YOU KNOW?** This scene features a quote from Anthony Bourdain's Travel Channel blog, accessed in January 2012.

## I'M NOT GOING TO ANSWER THAT

Leonardo diCaprio sneaks onto a movie set, steals a pair of knock-off Ray Bans from the night market and suddenly becomes less of himself.

He's just an extra. No presh. Not even visible.

Economy Class crams him in up against the bathroom, with a great view of the curtained-off First Class cabin and its spectacular In-Flight Service.

Watching "Hidden Hobbit, Crouching Masturbator" on his iPhone, he discovers that fan sites and Facebook don't lie. Harry Potter and Frodo Baggins got sex appeal, and _they're_ invisible men.

The celebrity in this scene doesn't even have to be me.

**TROUBLE IN FOREIGN COUNTRY: INFORMATION BOOKLET**

CLAIRE DANES: In the layout I made them believe I had integrity, that I could suffer needlessly to redeem my character. In this shitty third world joke, I cut the cassette with smack and fake Rolexes, smuggle padded bras with cockroaches and gold Buddhas. We don't do dick but pick grass in an illusion, rock the casbah of raw sewage. Girls from Ohio mention Thailand in beer bottle delerium and buy each other bracelets.

It was as simple as that.

INFORMATION: This scene steals effects from the movie *Brokedown Palace*; "delerium" refers to the band of the same name, who has a song on its soundtrack.

# DELETED SCENE

## THE KING OF THE WHITE ELEPHANT

Tony Jaa runs up a million flights of stairs in Sydney to train. He watches his elephant take a shit on a map of America before meeting the King who made up white elephant gift exchanges.

All he gets from that party is a dollar.

**DID YOU KNOW?** This title is taken from the 1940 Thai historical drama. The author once attended a holiday party in which a White person read from a book about the Thai origins of "white elephant" gift-giving. All the author got from that gift exchange was a $1 bill.

**MISTY MALARKY YING YANG**
Owned by Amy Carter, Jimmy Carter's daughter

Dear Misty Malarky Ying Yang,

Your name is too long.

Dear Misty Malarky Ying Yang,

Daughters of US presidents love Siamese cats! Did you ever meet Shan Shein, owned by Susan Ford, daughter of Gerald? You might have gotten along and been close friends. So close you could have been twins!

Haha.

Dear Misty Malarky Ying Yang,

The Malarky would have been enough. Misty would have been too tame. And Ying, Yang, or Ying Yang together is just a stereotype. Poor cat, you have too many names. What did Amy call you in the privacy of her presidential girlhood?

My, my. She called you "mine."

Dear M.M.Y.Y. (sorry for the abbrev. it's just easier :) thx),

The origins of your kind are unknown, but are believed to be Thai. And when you believe yourself to be Thai, you are Thai! That's what people on YouTube say. Your breed was one of the most popular breeds in Europe and North America.

I bet it is because you are white.

## SAGAT'S_ENDING.MP3

Street Fighter II Sagat is the final kill in this Southeast Asian
port city.

Francoise Sagat is pushing one of six buttons in an arterial
arcade,

arched around his guts like a band shell amphitheater chedi
in his one dead eye.

Bald heads sweat slicked. The guns are toy, the money fake,
the music MIDI.


Street Fighter II Sagat is a boss level, the backdrop:
Thailand.

Francoise Sagat enters the challenger's side.

Despite the 2D playing field, both show remarkable versatility.

Controls are unlocked. They try to KO at the same time.


Street Fighter II Sagat wanders Folsom Street Fair rocking a
glowing scar.

Francoise Sagat pushes the scar and it disappears. When
they fuck

it glows underneath, his shorts change colors, and his skin
turns a darker shade.

Sometimes he sees out of one eye. Sometimes, the other.

# PRIVATE EYE: DIARY OF
# A LONELY ASSASSIN

*private eye in the booth*    *[surveillance]*
*private i on the page*    *[confessional poetry]*
*privates on which i have my eye*    *[voyeurism]*

## NO OFFENSE INTENDED

in the voice of Christopher Lee as villain Scaramanga in
*The Man With The Golden Gun* (1974)

*i am an actor who loved to play a part*
*but then forgot who i really was.*
*White men put me in the jungle, in charge*
*of primitive people, and gave me absolute*
*power over them. they watched me perform magic,*
*call in air strikes and saw rice and guns fall*

*from the sky. they believed i was some sort of fallen god*, but
i'm just a Private Eye and Closet Poet, part Lonely Assassin
in a magical paradise unprepared to return to the way it
was, constructing a theatrical funhouse for The Perfect Kill,
sponsored by Absolut Vodka. i walk 20 paces to the corner
7Eleven; they charge

10 bucks for 8 oz. of KC Masterpiece BBQ Sauce. you only live
once when you're in charge, and even though i'm invisible on
an island in Thailand, i still fall down in a Jumbo Jump full
of jasmine rice and Walther PPKs and jump up in absolute
joy, my houseboy in a suitcase watching through the Security
Camera. this is the part i really like: i get into the shower with
a pistol. was that my third nipple? when women in bikinis hit
master overrides with their butts, magic

**HIGHLIGHTS:** This diary entry features a quote by former head of CIA Bill Lair in reference to Tony Poe, as cited by Jerry Hopkins in "The Real Colonel Kurtz?" in *Bangkok Babylon* (Tuttle Publishing, 2005, page 21). Tony Poe is rumored to be the inspiration for the character played by Marlon Brando in *Apocalypse Now*. The quote has been modified from the original, with pronouns and point-of-view changed.

**DID YOU KNOW?** There are also references from the James Bond film *The Man With The Golden Gun* (1974) and John Burdett's novel *Bangkok 8* (Alfred A. Knopf, New York, 2003). Burdett writes in a disclaimer: "This is an entertainment within a very Western genre, and nothing more. No offense is intended."

tends to happen. i'm no practitioner of magic, but i want to create a Masterpiece charged with solar energy. video rolling: this was my long lost calling—acting—and the repertoire for the fall season repeats itself in a hall of mirrors. in part two of the feature film, i serve absolute

crime novel realness, in a Massage-Internet-Coffee-Steak-Out with an absolutely tropic twist: snakes, whores and nirvana like a magician copping a cop's life—undercover surveillance, shooting body parts in parked cars, looking over Top Secret files, while my charge takes a nap anywhere without falling. if this was

a mystery, how would The Author build it? The Staged Death was both the first and last scenes. i admire the absolute persistence of the middle as it begins to fall off a bridge and then magically come back to life, like a charging line of soldiers learning lines and parts.

my part to play was as entertainment
in a very Western genre. i took charge of absolutes
and like cryptic magic, fell.

## ERASE EVERY TRACE
in the voice of Nicolas Cage as hit man Joe in
*Bangkok Dangerous* (2008)

*it takes an emotional resilience to be on the outside,*
*year after year, required by law to leave*
*the country every three months for a new visa.*
*that may sound like a small thing, but it gives life a bite,*
*a spin. concessions must be made. dreams*
*and desires are changed and shaped.*

i sit down to play chess in a white tuxedo as the drama takes shape. my opponent is a deaf-mute girl who works at a pharmacy. i stand outside looking in. small glass vials clack against the counter like knights dreaming of pawns. i want to manipulate the material and leave, impose some order, but Bangkok bites. here i will eventually break all my rules. for example, my heart is already accidentally visaed,

lines stamped and drawn, a 2-color print-out. all my clothes, cash, credit cards, and paper visas fold up into passports—in silence i decide which country will take my shape, which metropolis will grant me anon. it doesn't matter that this is a remake; i bite my tongue and say to the customs agent, "holiday," never taking an interest in people outside of work. emotional attachments leave only sacrifice and abrupt cine-matic ends to dreams

**DID YOU KNOW?** This diary entry features a quote by Christopher Moore regarding the expat life, cited by Jerry Hopkins in *Bangkok Babylon* (99). It references Nicolas Cage's character in the 2008 remake of the original *Bangkok Dangerous* (1999) Thai film. In the original, the deaf-mute character is the hit man, but in the remake, Cage's love interest is the deaf mute. The reference to chess is taken from the Murray Head music video to "One Night in Bangkok," which was a song written for the musical *Chess* (1984/1986).

i allowed myself to want. in the original, my dream girl speaks and i am a deaf mute. without a visa to enter her world, i am stuck within a country i cannot leave. it begins and ends in silence, a breakage that shapes sinew and severs it from bone, separating feeling outside of action—blown up, bitten.

i am impenetrable on a black BMW K1200R, but what bites into the consciousness of this lonely assassin is a dream: a kid with jasmine flower, fragile in the alley, interrupting my getaway. outside, numbers are uneven, i'm always a split second too late, visas expire in my pocket. the shape of my future has upturned the elephant's trunk. the unlucky often leave

in search of another chance, so i cross the border again. leave. try to speak to the girl who can't hear me. and when i take a bite of my target, i imagine the gunshot naked, a silent picture. death takes shape not with sound, but with its silence, and when i dream i have no ears, no mouth. i ask for a visa to her heart. she smiles and collects her things outside.

on the outside i can leave,
come again on a new visa, bite
but never taste the dream's silent shape.

## MY POEM IS...THE WORLD ACCORDING TO SAGAT

Three Sagats are hiding in an arcade. One is just a player pushing pennies, toy guns, and paper money. The battle doesn't start until you press select, and if you get to the end you'll unlock the boss's backdrop—there's a King for everything. *Continue...?*

You push every possible combination of 6 buttons. Sagat delivers his commands (run.exe). He ranks as an obstruction and an exception. While the credits roll you rifle for change in order to return to the site of the final kill. By then, credit card readers have replaced coin-op slots and playable character Sagat is on a level all his own, the Top of the Asian Underworld, ranking underground in a temple ruin. Cue wooden flute and snake.

Sagat starts rapping in the arch-filled passageway. Arterial arcades and cerebral programming continue to crash. Sagat doesn't have an ending, although he predictably becomes the end of all. His character is unlockable, credited to a Cherokee actor and a White actor wearing a Cherokee bandana. Sagat continues to ask questions and say, *man, fuck that, get outta my face*, a playwright on the street corner while the other two fight.

They start to emulate each other by wearing eye patches. Rankings show Sagat has more points bottoming to the boss who can put him in his rank. One says to two, *You fuck like* a *video* game when it's almost ended <Hold R and push A & B at the same time> <Lightly tap C> When he starts to come all his scars glow.

His shorts say *Tiger* and yours say *Yes*, not to discredit the climax of the night. An iconic chest wound plays out in select versions, voiced in Japanese and English. Sagat's eye patch continually switches sides, his tiny shorts switch colors and his scar continues to disappear.

Second in command to a Bison, ranked #11 in the Top 25, a new challenger comes out to play on the bonus stage. It's all about his appearance in the end and the way he can be defeated without too much difficulty, credited as the Best Scarred Character for everything the scar starts to symbolize.

In the arcade all three Sagats start a 3-way. One alternates as a game console. Hit continue. It's just an elephant. No wait, it's Kylie Minogue taking the credit for 4 years of ROTC, Swiss bank accounts and stealth mode, moving up in the ranks. *I love Kylie*, says Sagat, *I love her music*. His ending .mp3 is being recorded, all that's left is revenge and Zagat ratings. REPLAY:

Player select Sagat starts, arcs the cadence, intercepts the end command like war, like software, like soft core. *Continue?* comes after you push, jump rank, and leave with all the credit.

# ONE NIGHT IN BANGKOK

*One night in Bangkok and the world's your oyster. The bars are temples but the pearls ain't free. You'll find a god in every golden cloister, and if you're lucky then the god's a she. A little flesh, a little history. One night in Bangkok makes a hard man humble, not much between despair and ecstasy. One night in Bangkok and the tough guys tumble, can't be too careful with your company. I can feel the devil walking next to me.*

Jeff Corwin was just bitten by a reticulated python and it hurts like the devil, but Nicolas Cage has come to Bangkok to die and wants to flirt with danger and go to temples, so they move through Thailand like a typhoon on Cage's hog-nosed bat, looking tough.

Bouncing around Cage like a drunken ballerina who's been cloistered with other very fragile mammals for much too long, Jeff is excited to share as many little surprises as possible. All Cage has to do is keep to four little rules and live out of a suitcase in an invisible world, but even that won't stay the devil.

Bangkok is any combination of three adjectives, and in it you can experience much of the world's Best Wildlife Encounters. Cage puts a gun to his temple while Jeff pretends to be pulled under. Hungover in a cloister, they're in a very special place in Thailand and since they're ignorant it's time to get tough:

**DID YOU KNOW?** This destination features lyrics to the song "One Night in Bangkok" from the musical *Chess*. Originally composed by former ABBA members, it was sung by Murray Head and covered by Robey, Danish boy band C21, Thai female pop group Silk, and more. It references Nicolas Cage's character in *Bangkok Dangerous*, *The Jeff Corwin Experience* episode on Thailand (Season 1 Episode 6 "The Royalty of Siam" [2000] Animal Planet) and the movie *The Hangover 2*, for which the tagline is: "Bangkok Has Them Now."

Jeff inserts his entire arm up an elephant's rectum and it's not tough at all. He pulls snakes out of the water, yelling, WHERE'S YOUR HEAD. Little by little tourists learn to flock to cloisters and cages.

Jeff and Cage take pictures with gibbons, devils armed with bananas. They go to a cocktail party in a temple and discover they both like durian. They ride a Ferris wheel too much and watch silent movies in the Charlie Chaplin Film Festival.

Without giving it much thought, Cage writes his mobile number on Jeff's forearm. Cage plays tough and hides in a warehouse full of water bottles, massages his temples and repeats rule #4: *Know when to get out*, which of course he breaks. Little do they know about *eye for eye* or *tooth for tooth* or what it feels like to have a devil enshrine the body.

Cage constructs a cloister in which his demon self can live. The only way it can survive is through mimicry and imitation. A cloistered life proves to be too much to handle. "It thinks it belongs here, this devil inside of me. It toughens up my insides so that all the big and little impossible, memorable things I will always, inevitably, forget." Drawing a gun in one temple and pointing the barrel to another, cloisters shatter. The freedom is a little too much to take.

"Bangkok, that tough devil, has me now."

# THE JUNGLE BOX

*[Jim Thompson] kept his pills in an antique silver box, given to him by one of his sisters, which friends in Bangkok had jokingly dubbed his "jungle box," since he had taken to carrying it with him whenever he went on trips upcountry.*

*[Mindreader Al] Koran had a depressing vision to report: Thompson, he said, had gone into the jungle like an elephant to find a secret place to die. "I felt this as strongly as I have felt anything in my life."*

*He was sitting in the chair...right there...he was not sitting in the house...the chair was on the veranda... [...]...he is not in the jungle...I want to follow the route where they picked him up...he was sitting right there...this chair...[...]*

**INFORMATION:** These epigraphs are from William Warren's book, pages 12, 166 and 179 respectively. The third epigraph is an excerpt from Dutch mystic Peter Hurkos' visions.

## TYCOON

Open on Jim walking in the jungle box: He holds a map in his hand. The legend depicts coordinates to popular landmarks. One of them is the body of a lone man walking in the jungle box: Jim.

By now Jim has made a career as a tour guide for new arrivals. He customizes splendor levels for each map and then gifts that map to a wandering stranger. Hypnotized by the glittering pulse of each destination, tourists become "jungle fever savvy," bragging that they know more than the jungle box offers at first sight—at beaten path—at lonely planet. Legends are made this way: Jim hypnotizes the strange arrivals and makes them believe they are all alone. By mass-producing the directions to Splendor, Jim is fast on his way to making another career for himself, if a career can be made out of Asia and a jungle full of dream people.

Jim empties three packets of Splenda into his iced coffee and watches the movie *Legend* on Netflix. Loneliness is one of the provinces he's come to enjoy, hypnotized by his own powers of self-invention. Undergoing regression hypnosis he puts his resume on Career-Builder.com, listing "Silk Tycoon" as his previous occupation, "Loner" as another, "Keeper of the Jungle Box" as a third, "Legendary American" as a fourth.

All the splendid wonders of the world, all the splendors of this place rise up and move the earth in a hypnotic dance, becoming a guidebook, a legend in the making. Jim changed careers, read every jungle book, built the jungle box alone as a place where expats can loan their bodies to die in the splendor that tsunamis most American dreams. "A rumbo in da jungo" is the soundtrack to desire, and Jim hypnotically captures the heart of every White man, inspiring within them careers of love for this land of legend.


The legend says "YOU ARE ALONE"—
your career of splendor begins at the X—
Jim hypnotizes you while the jungle box awakes.

# MAUGHAM

In the jungle box Jim encounters W. Somerset Maugham, a rare creature. The strangeness of his demeanor is somewhat lost on Jim, whose theatre stars the British and the Native, but no one so perplexing as the Homosexual.

Somerset is after the preservation of his suite at The Oriental: he wants it clean as a novel—each thread of each silk sheet pressed and set. He's writing a new posthumous novel, now that he's dead and taken up residence in the jungle box. It will be a rare book indeed, published on white fronds of elephant grass and preserved in the oral tradition of the brown race.

The presence of his lover Haxton offers no strangeness. The overall climate in the jungle box is more perplexed at Jim's adamant inclusion of a theatre on the premises, with a different play put up each evening. Jim is fond of theatrical demonstrations; he demands his home be like a novel in its architectural embellishments and picturesque surroundings. He invents and perplexes any crowd that comes to call.

Somerset makes a rare request of The Oriental. Strange, he asks for his adjoining rooms to be preserved as *The Jim Thompson Suite*. Preservation has long been one of Jim's chief careers, a theatre within which he has engaged much of his strange expertise and cultural knowledge. "I'll purchase all the novels White man has written on Thailand and found a rare books annex and study," was Jim's perplexing decision. Somerset always wanted other people to sleep in

**DID YOU KNOW?** There is actually a Somerset Maugham suite in The Oriental Hotel (also briefly referred to in the "One Night in Bangkok" song) [http://www.famoushotels.org/article/698].

his bed, perplexed was he that the idea didn't thrill Jim, who had a leaning more toward the preservation of fact than he was of fiction.

Jim decorates the rare books annex with five white heads and writes a theatre play entitled "The Episode of the Five White Heads," which features in Somerset's novel, "The Twelve Meanings of Escape." Any strangeness between them soon dries out, as strangeness is wont to be rid of its own perplexing proclivities and roll itself out narratively as a novel would, straight and clean, at least in print. Somerset's durian preserves deck the breakfast table of his suite, a theatre in which all who stay become lost.

Rarer and rarer still is the stranger Haxton, left out of Somerset and Jim's theatre, perplexed but preserved like a novel (untouched) idea.

Jim Thompson encounters Jerry Hopkins in the jungle box, an authority and drinking buddy to every White male expat who's sought color in Bangkok Babylon. At The Oriental Hotel Jerry Hopkins' room is across the hall from Jim and Somerset's suites. Over scotch they share sentiments of Adventure and Romance and the stages upon which these were set. Every evening was a variety show, they reminisce. Jerry chose Bangkok for its rich variety of possibility and the people, who are as friendly as the Tourism Authority says. Jim and Somerset can't help but sympathize, although at this stage in the game they are disappointed in Jerry's color palette and why he failed to include them in his book. They're getting sentimental for 1926 and 1957. Jim and Somerset have entire suites in this hotel named after them. Who does this Jerry guy think he is? This hotel deserves to put up more legendary guests than him, people with actual variety in their desires for re-invention. *My sentiments exactly*, chirps Somerset, eyeing Jerry's authority and his writing style, which lacks much refinement and is, to say the least, "colorful" and full of colorful characters taking the stage.

Jerry explains, "I got on a plane with three suitcases and landed on stage at the Babylon Bangkok Bed & Breakfast— it might almost have been called a hotel—in a colorful gay foam party." Jim nods and Somerset almost chokes, surprised at the variety he just added to the play. Jerry used to be a journalist, so he knows how to authorize in a headline the theatrics of a particular sentiment. Jim and Somerset are beginning to feel a bit sentimental again, now that they're dead, and like Jerry they are all staging their deaths here in the Jungle Black Box Theatre. The death of the author is

**DID YOU KNOW?** The only reason the author found out about Jerry Hopkins was because he appeared on Anthony Bourdain's Thailand episode. Hopkins' book is *Bangkok Babylon*, but Babylon Bangkok is a gay bed and breakfast hotel.

being filmed right here in the Somerset Maugham suite of The Oriental Hotel; malaria and fairy stories add a splash of variety when they have nothing else to do but color in the lines. Jerry tells his own colorful story in 3rd person; even though it is sentimental it still manages to re-invent itself. Jerry eats a variety of fish on-screen with Anthony Bourdain to boost his amazon.com ratings. The stage manager asks Jerry to autograph his book. Back at the hotel, Jerry expounds on his authority of escape. Authorizing the local color "to get away, as from confinement," like a hotel full of sentiments he checks out late and shoves the rest on stage, for variety.

# NOONE

In the jungle box Jim encounters imperial ethnographer Pat NOONE, exotic as any novelist's creation, permanently living with "the monkeys" in a museum, as it were, and noting sexual fetishes and bowel movements as fact, when only fiction can save him, something much more imaginative than observation or the empirical truth. Imagination is much more powerful than most believe; as Jim knows, the exotic is merely a transformation of what was once bland in an effort to save itself.

Pat NOONE has constructed a permanent encampment in the jungle box with the bones of the native wife who killed him. Facts fall out of his hands when once the ink held. His life has become a museum with strangers peering in on all sides. But in the jungle box a museum is exactly what Jim aims to build. He can imagine that those who escape to Thailand and choose not to return, who in fact fake their own deaths, would want to exoticize themselves in a permanent state of re-invention, and believe that they are saved.

Jim knows that NOONE wants to be saved by something larger, seeks to idolize himself in a museum of curiosities, longs for the permanence afforded by the possession of a dream image, imagines forgetting himself and adorning his body with exotic things like a temple—all these factor into the landmark Jim will build, the fact of its existence held up by its future savings. NOONE is reminded of The Dream People's exotic dances, and how Jim Thompson's home is now a museum, and that to be imaginative one must let go of the idea that anything is permanent.

**DID YOU KNOW?** Pat Noone was a British anthropologist who studied the Temiah (Senoi) or "Dream People," indigenous to Upper Perak in Malaysia [http://www2. ucsc.edu/dreams/Library/senoi2.html]. Coincidentally, he disappeared in the same jungle as Jim Thompson. The author is interested in reading his name as "no one."

Somerset and Haxton get matching perms. NOONE Googles factual evidence to back up his research claims. "IMAGI-NATION" spray-paints the jungle box paths. Jim makes a trip to Save-A-Lot to stock up on supplies for his human museum: an exhibition of White men who found the exotic a nicer place to die than America. These exotic bodies are part of Jim's permanent collection, on exhibit in the Jungle Box Museum, full of facts but mostly fictive offerings to the savior they imagine.

# THE GOLDEN BANANA

Stopping off at many of the places he had used so effectively as backgrounds for his stories and novels, Somerset encounters his love for faraway ruins and hunger and nightmare memories, when Bangkok still retained much of its glamour (no air con, no gas stove). Jim preferred the European name Siam, ripe with nostalgia with its spicy scents and its waterfront houses from an alien culture.

In a game of charades Jim plays a silk merchant pursued by intelligence agents in a nightclub called The Golden Banana. The next day FBI agents show up in indigenous disguises searching for UFOs. They run background checks on all residents to determine who among them are alien-human hybrids, at which point touring expats will be detained and exported faraway from here. During their internment in America they will create an arrested nostalgia for the jungle box in their dreams.

Coy decoys Somerset and Haxton heighten the glamour of the police state situation by hosting a glamourous drag ball. They sew silk garters and brooches out of lychee and longan to distract the federal agents and bury within them a nostalgic longing to cross-dress underneath their black suits and cross fade into the background...to be discovered again 50 odd years later when psychics unearth Unidentified Faraway Objects to display in Jim's Jungle Box Museum.

Jim doesn't believe in aliens, he believes we are indeed alone on this lonely planet. Somerset believes in the alien concept that "by travel I can add to my personality and so glamour myself a little, putting on my face, transporting myself faraway into the jungle box where the agents won't be able to find me."

Haxton begins to paint landscapes and in the background appear shadows of UFOs and his new self, nostalgically reclined in a lawn of rambutan. This color is called Nostalgia and his nails are painted with it. Haxton's aliens approach from out of the foliage, his background becomes worn and diffuse, a glamourous portrait just visible through the white fog.

The travel agency has closed its doors. Too many people want to die in this faraway place called the jungle box, it's too easy to find a far-off armchair traveling clone nowadays. Nostalgia is much more vivid than a hotel. And so the agents read Somerset's novels in the de-briefing room while the aliens continue to elude them, back in the future where Glamour is a magazine and Thailand is a background singer in a novel on the Kindle, featuring Jim's background as a faraway escape artist, Somerset's glamour as gay, pop nostalgia, and Haxton's aliens as special agents investigating fake deaths.

## JIM THOMPSON, BANGKOK

He had become a sort of landmark himself, a personality so widely known, though he read every available book on the region, there are too many relatively safe ways to dispose of a person in Asia, since it has no clearly defined center and there is almost as much pleasure in seeming to be behind the scenes, as in being behind them,

that a letter addressed simply TO: JIM THOMPSON, BANG-KOK found its way to him in a city of 3.5 million people, TO: GPS or Google Earth as a municipality translated into a play, he is a plot of land marked with gaffing tape instead of numbers, sketched as a series of scenes illustrated in a guidebook (read: novel), he is the center-justified title of a stage adaptation of a disposable city, THE TWELVE MEAN-INGS OF ESCAPE.

Jim directs 12 modern dance students, disposing of his own body as a character. He longs to pull the curtains and strike the set, TO: mark stage center-center with a glow-in-the-dark X, to construct a landmark out of three suitcases that the dancers then dismantle and manipulate. They read from W. Somerset Maugham's *The Gentleman in the Parlour* and reenact random scenes at twelve minute intervals. Each scene must incorporate the three suitcases and the disposal of a body. In the play Jim enters a novel and reads himself to the dancers, who lyricize his disappearance. TO: enter a novel requires transferring the body into language, into a landmark that can be used to mark the page.

In the absence of a central figure, THE TWELVE MEANINGS OF ESCAPE centralizes twelve scenes, each defined by a hidden landmark that the twelve dancers must uncover and dispose of during the duration of the performance. TO: watch Jim's play is to read his ineffable presence in the text, but to discover that the escaped body is unreadable—at the center but not centered—addressed TO: a final scene that remains unwritten, an epilogue that has been disposed and replaced with a landmark.

He had become the sort of landmark you read about in books, one of many White men who were lost, disposed, but who still occupy the center of scenes TO: which we are inexplicably drawn.

# THE TWELVE MEANINGS OF ESCAPE

*Jim...Jim...*

*You've got to come with us to Babylon...BKK...B&B ...*

Somerset and his partner Haxton are in the clearing eating rambutan.

Piles of soft hairy shells litter the lawn. Fingernails dig to break open skin.

Massaged, crab-band plastic-sandaled feet brush pink-red shells and lime green tentacle tips like loofah.

Somerset and Haxton are half naked on white wicker.

Pink-red skins and sauna steam.

White rambutan fruit slips into mouths, white terry cloth towels slip.

Fronds draped about their secrets.

**HIGHLIGHTS:** This title references Jerry Hopkins, who closes his book *Bangkok Babylon* with the following: "This is a book that celebrates bumpy Bangkok and the concept of escape. My dictionary has twelve meanings next to the word 'escape.' The first one says, 'to get away, as from confinement.' That does it for me and, I think, everyone else in this book" (224). It also references the first 12 things that came up when the author Googled "escape." The italicized line in 1: and 8: is a play on the Enrique Iglesias song, "Escape." 6: uses another excerpt of Hurkos' visions, via Warren. "In Search of the Dream People" references Noone.

**DID YOU KNOW?** This piece was written while listening to Kronos Quartet's *White Man Sleeps* album (1987).

Jim pushes them back.


Haxton turns on the fog machine. The sauna rattles.

Somerset and Haxton are enveloped by a smoothie of Eurasian voices and mulatto dogs.

Leaning forward in his wicker and terry, Haxton dangles a pocket watch of silver sterling before Jim's face.


Under hypnosis, Jim dreams of the different ways he could die.

I am on a plane with three suitcases...I am a crashed military UFO...I am a white man sleeps...I am sitting on a chair...right here...I am not sitting in the house...the chair is on the verandah...I am walking down the road...I am walking like an elephant into the jungle to find a secret place to die...

## 1: DEATH BY HIT SINGLE

Jim's international #1 hit single: "In Search Of The
Dream People"

*All the secrets are kept here*
*The secrets only a foreigner would know*
*I just wanted a secret place to die that NOONE would know*

*The dream people wisk us away*
*I leave my body and forget myself*
*I find a new one, I find NOONE*
*NOONE in the jungle box can save me*

*I am captured by the dream*
*Captured by the dream people*
*The romance of the dream lured me in*
*And fed me the fruit of escape*

*I uncovered secrets*
*I found a new self*
*I could run as far as I wanted*
*I could leave myself*

*And there I will be left alone*
*Everyone finds their own place in time*
*And when I run far enough*
*I'll find my secret place to die*

*You can run you can hide but you can't escape my jungle x8*

## 2: DEATH BY GUIDEBOOK

On the path Jim runs into Joe Cummings, the Lonely Planet guy.

A giant pile of *Lonely Planet Thailand* guidebooks—every single print edition copy that has ever existed—obscures the path. They are all open to the entry on the Jim Thompson House.

Joe is flipping through each book. Every once and a while he mumbles something inaudible to an invisible intern.

Jim touches these books. He's disappeared in them a million times.

Jim points to an entry. "That's me," he says.

Joe Cummings looks up.

Jim is squashed by the sheer quantity and cumulative weight of these books. They open up their bindings and chomp down on Jim's tasty limbs.

## 3: DEATH BY UFO

On the path Jim runs into a UFO. The insignia on the craft's side is "ESC." The UFO has made itself visible in order to abduct him. *This is a nicer way to die*, the ship communicates via telepathy. *It's easy to get lost in the jungle box, but NOONE will know.* Aliens on board hand Jim an iPad. The window shows a program by which he can fake his own death.

Jim considers for a moment, then hits escape.

## 4: DEATH BY DANCE

Jim gets up and dances with Somerset and Haxton on the lawn with the furry rambutan skins and the fronds, pink-green, barefoot until their towels slip. He wants to go with them to Babylon BKK B&B and have tea in their suite with the rambutan shells piled around. They peel their towels and then their hairy skins.

The flesh underneath is white.

## 5: DEATH BY PSYCHIC

Jim runs into a mob of psychics on the path. They're all trying to read his mind at once. The amount of psychic energy crushes his brain, and Jim collapses.

## 6: DEATH BY TRUCK

*...one vehicle, like a military vehicle...like a truck...I see truck...ah, truck, about from here on the road...he walks down the road...*

"Get in the truck."

I'll do anything to avoid going home again.

## 7: DEATH BY TIGER

Jim sips a cup of tea and Haxton turns on the gramophone.

Out of the gramophone leaps a Tiger.

The Tiger and Jim dance and pounce about.

Their pounces become muffled.

The Tiger's teeth come down

like a paper cutter.

## 8: DEATH BY ESCAPE

The box is open.

All the creatures of the jungle come tumbling out
and my new self rushes forth with a machete,
                        with the jaws of a tiger,
                        with a truck and 14 people,
to take me.

I want to be taken.

It's funny, in the jungle box you can escape to live forever.
But I escaped here to find a secret place to die.

I won't stop until I find it.

*You can run you can hide but you can't escape my jungle x8*

## 9: DEATH BY TREE SPIRIT

Jim stumbles into the Tree Spirit, who rattles.
They dance.
The Tree Spirit sings.

*[rattle]*          Let me have you, Jim
Let me weave you up
Let me dance you to thread, Jim
Let me unspool you, limb and sinew

*[rattle]*          Let your gold feed my old roots
and trucks, so I may bear juicy fruits
Let me gut you
into the fabric of my dreams

*[rattle]*          Let me add this and this color
this and this twig
Let me Thai you to me,
into the fiber of my bark

*[rattle]*          Tree Spirit loves you. It wants to keep you.
It wants to secrete you here.
Tuck-tuck in among the twigs
to wait hidden like war taut.

*[rattle]*          There are much easier ways to die.

## 10: DEATH BY ART HISTORY

On the path Jim has a massive head injury and losses consciousness, going into a coma.

> He is compelled to get an MA in Thai language and art history.
> He teaches English in Surin, the elephant capital.
> He acquires a new Thai wife, who he describes as "an incredible cook."
> He hopes to adopt a Siamese cat.
> He authors many books on the subject.
> He contemplates getting Thai citizenship and a Ford Escape SUV.

Luckily, none of these things take as long as they would in real life.

Twenty seconds later, Jim emerges from his coma rich with experiences, memories and feelings, but without credentials.

This is what he builds his new life around.

## 11: DEATH BY WHITE ELEPHANT

On the path, Jim runs into The White Elephant.

The White Elephant is in the middle of a paintball match.

Splotches of color that have missed their target splatter the trees around him.

> *Hey, NOONE is supposed to find me.*
> *NOONE is supposed to know about this place.*
>
> *Well, here you are...gone like an elephant into the jungle to find a secret place to die?*
> *You'll be MY secret now.*

And in that moment, when Jim turned to face the elephant,
in that moment, when his sight met his eye,
in that moment, when that blue dot started to bleed,

The White Elephant knew that Jim's body would never be found.

## 12: DEATH BY DREAM

Hypnotized by the rhythmic sound of the pounce and the rising warmth of the steam, Jim begins to fall asleep.

White men full of escape gently touch him on the shoulder and waist.

They lift him up and carry him short distances, releasing him down to the ground soundlessly.

Jim is the common point of contact they share.

White terry cloth knotted to their waists,

they are balletic in their serious attention to working together,

their breath creating the needed heat.


It's a dance theatre piece

and Somerset is in the audience writing it all down in a novel.

Haxton is eating buttered popcorn, entranced.

Somerset's fingertips are poised, typing hunt and peck on his iPad.

> dot dot dot shift I space
> f-o-u-n-d space a space n-e-w space
> s-e-l-f dot dot dot space

# THE GENTLEMAN
# IN THE PAGODA

*In one way or another, I've used in my writings pretty well
everything that has happened to me in the course of my life.
Sometimes an experience of my own has provided me with an
idea and I've just had to invent the incidents to illustrate it. But
more often I've taken people whom I've known, either slightly
or intimately, and used them as a foundation for characters of
my own invention. To tell you the truth, fact and fiction are so
intermingled in my work, that now looking back, I can hardly
distinguish one from the other.*

- W. Somerset Maugham

**HIGHLIGHTS:** Sample the delights of W. Somerset Maugham's *The Gentleman in
the Parlour: A record of a journey from Rangoon to Haiphong* (1930) in a fresh
and modern context. These destinations feature lines from Maugham's book, as
well as lines from Anna Leonowens' books that are ventriloquized by Irene Dunne,
who played Anna in *Anna and the King of Siam* (1946). The epigraph to this
section is taken from Maugham's preface to the film *Quartet 1948*, in which four
of Maugham's short stories are turned into films. The author is interested in the
ways Thailand becomes not a place or a people, but a piece of artwork, an object,
a painting or film or book—how easily it becomes fictionalized; Maugham and
Leonowens made many references to this in their writing.

# PREFACE

It was nothing to me but a name. Only as I went along did it gain a meaning and with a meaning, mystery. It had subdued suggestions on which the imagination might work and now it had a strangely romantic air.

Preparing you to enter into the state of mind proper to such an experience is the immense difficulty of getting there.

I did not care. It seemed to me that I had never arrived anywhere in such a romantic style and I could not but think that this must be the preface to an experience that would be memorable.

I had bought such stores as seemed necessary, folding chairs and a table, a filter, lamps and I know not what.

The casual acquaintance whose words spoken at random had tempted me to make the journey approached me now with a book.

SOMERSET is lounging in a dressing gown in his study, surrounded by books, each an escape. The literature that is kept in the jungle is rough with dashes, and as SOMERSET reads he replaces them with elegant semicolons and discreet brackets.

He begins his journey by reading a book that provides such a vivid experience, especially this passage here:

[Though the reader skips the passage it gives him a slight thrill of self-esteem to know that he is reading a book with solid fact in it.]

SOMERSET drops the book and is flooded with memories and recollections he had quite forgotten.

"When I write, these men on my shelves speak to me; they gossip amongst each other and whisper. I have put them down in such a way with words that they cannot escape the binding. They are forever bound, and bound men are better for conversation."

There is little information here, just words strung together for language's sake.

He takes a book off the shelf and opens it has he would a casual acquaintance.

# MUSEUM: A LECTURE ON TIME

IRENE DUNNE and SOMERSET sit on a bench watching landscape paintings. Each painting is a window. A video. A book.

As curators of The American Museum of Thai National Character's permanent retrospective, they often make special trips to visit the exhibit and take a look at the many breath-taking landscapes they've chosen to display.

Walking through these galleries, they feel strangely on the verge, pulled in.

IRENE: You know, I reluctantly quit this painting; it has impressed me with a feeling I can't analyze; it seems as if I am removed to some awful distance from the world I know, even more remotely excluded from any participation in its real life.

SOMERSET: I feel the same way. In this gallery, I seem to myself like a figure in a tapestry, an exact painting of which would be looked upon with incredulity, or as an invention of fairyland.

IRENE: I want to form in my mind's eye some picture of the lives those people led, to make the picture complete. They make such attractive little pictures that I would willingly have lingered in the accuracy and picturesque vividness of their fairytale.

SOMERSET: This one is an illustration based on a photograph, is it not?

IRENE: Yes. In a box, a girl in a photo against a backdrop, soft like the silk of old dresses in a museum.

SOMERSET: We watch landscapes like a poem, you and I; figures sink into the backcloth.

IRENE: She might have been a golden idol, given the period, or duration.

# THEATRE: A LECTURE ON CHANCE

*The Play:*

IRENE says *I feel as though I already knew Siam. I read a book once. Don't laugh.*

IRENE takes a seat next to SOMERSET in the very last row of The Theatre.

They watch a dress rehearsal for a performance art piece.

The entire piece happens behind a closed door.

IRENE puts on her opera glasses to get a better look.

She likes the illusion of being closer.

*The Commentary:*

IRENE: You're a critic, aren't you?

SOMERSET: Yes, in fact I'm writing a review of tonight's show for *The Times*. I usually write novels so I thought this would be a challenge. Actually, it's no different.

IRENE: Is that so?

SOMERSET: The story is as much the audience's own invention as it is the actor's. An actor brings to life a character based on an actual person who was, at one point in time, written into the page. (Pause.) You're the actor in this piece, aren't you?

IRENE: Yes. I ask myself the question over and over again, *Is it possible that I could be acting?*

SOMERSET: Anything is possible here. Is it *impossible* that you could be acting?

IRENE: Well, no, not that I know of.

SOMERSET: Then it's possible, isn't it?

IRENE: I often sit in the back row on opening night and watch myself. I watch myself being watched by the audience.

SOMERSET: And what do you believe? Is theatre much different than the pictures?

IRENE: I'm a reproduction of a real person. I'm a vast sun-drenched plain, a fit scene for the pageant of this ever-recurring drama.

SOMERSET: Then I sit here as one of your props, taking notes—a small decoration, an anti-climax.

IRENE: Tell me, does this play interest you? Have you found enough for your review?

SOMERSET: I will never have enough, but what I have will do.

IRENE: So, will you invent the rest?

SOMERSET: It will probably come to that, yes. It may even be the best part of this play, the part I invent.

IRENE: And tomorrow night, when the audience comes to The Theatre looking for that part? Will they be dissatisfied?

SOMERSET: No matter what the audience sees on this stage, they will always be able to find it.

IRENE: What are the chances?

*The Criticism*

"The Twelve Meanings of Escape"
is a complicated but monotonous
variation on a single theme. It is as
good as a play and doubtless much
better than most. It is completely
unimaginative. It has no reality;
there is something stagy about it.
The effect is charmingly unreal.
The character of the scene had
been changing, but it had been so
gradual that I had scarcely noticed
it. It has not the beauty of nature,
but of theatre.

## PAGODA: A LECTURE ON MUTABILITY

Each pagoda opens roads down which the imagination can make many a careless and unexpected journey. Each is a labyrinth in which I cannot find my way.

I come across a pagoda stuck over with little white flags. Even though this one is nearly identical to the hundreds of others I have seen on my journey, there is something different about this one. It gives me a strange feeling I have never felt before.

Or it could be that, after the lapse of years, having become a different person, I can in this pagoda see a structure of brick and whitewash that has only just been erected, that has only just crossed over from the fairy realm, that has only just been uncovered by the first rays of light.

The ruins of this pagoda offer peculiar sensations that I find curious to expose myself to. It is huge, it is crowded, it dazzles the eyes and takes the breath away, it is empty, it is dead, you wander about a trifle disconsolate.

After all, it means nothing to me.

I stumble upon a ritual performance. The dancers dance around the pagoda in whiteface, their hands like rare and fantastic orchids. No emotion, no fleeting thought is permitted to disturb the immobility of their expression.

I approach the inner niche of the pagoda. As I get closer, I receive the greatest shock of all.

I see myself, my body, mummified in gold leaf like a golden idol.

I lie there, panting and sleepless. Shapes of monstrous pagodas throng my brain and great gilded Buddhas bear down on me.

This new self is much too human.

To give a character in one of my novels my flesh and bones is more real, more palpable, than pressing bits of gold leaf to my head, arms, legs.

From now on it is I that lives in a book,

while my character sits in that pagoda,

stirred by my blood,

watching the ruin with unchanged eye.

Some pieces previously appeared in slightly different versions: "One Night in Bangkok" in *OCHO*; "The White Elephant Ride" in *Eleven Eleven*; "The Romance of the Siamese Dream" in *EOAGH* and *learning to loveDANCEmore*.

Other sources include Anna Harriette Leonowens' *The English Governess at the Siamese Court: Being Recollections of Six Years in the Royal Palace at Bangkok* (Oxford University Press, Oxford, 1988) and *Siamese Harem Life* (E.P. Dutton & Company, Inc, New York, 1953); Margaret Landon's *Anna and the King of Siam* (John Day Company, New York, 1944); and Susan Morgan's *Bombay Anna: The Real Story and Remarkable Adventures of the King and I Governess* (University of California Press, Berkeley, 2008).